BORDERS AND DISTRICTS

IN

BIBLICAL HISTORIOGRAPHY

JERUSALEM BIBLICAL STUDIES

edited by

Ora Lipschitz and Alexander Rofé

The "Jerusalem Biblical Studies" aims at publishing a series of monographs on biblical literature and its formation, the religion of Israel and ancient Near Eastern history.

BORDERS AND DISTRICTS

IN

BIBLICAL HISTORIOGRAPHY

SEVEN STUDIES

IN BIBLICAL GEOGRAPHICAL LISTS

by

Nadav Na'aman

Simor Ltd.
Jerusalem 1986

JERUSALEM BIBLICAL STUDIES

1. A. Rofe, "The Book of Balaam" (Numbers 22:2-24:25). [Hebrew]
2. T. Rudin-O'brasky, The Patriarchs in Hebron and Sodom (Genesis 18-19). [Hebrew]
3. E. Tov, The Text-Critical Use of the Septuagint in Biblical Research.

Simor Ltd.
POBox 39039, Tel Aviv 61390
ISBN 965-242-005-0

Printed in Israel
at the Yuval Press, Jerusalem

TABLE OF CONTENTS

LIST OF MAPS

PREFACE

This book developed gradually out of my increasing interest in the geographical lists of the Bible. The study of this subject has generally focused on one of two main aspects: the location of isolated toponyms or groups of toponyms mentioned in the lists, or the clarification of complete lists.

The identification of biblical toponyms throughout the Land of Israel has been greatly simplified over the years, and has resulted in scores, even hundreds, of articles, which have notably advanced our understanding of the lists.

The interpretation of the comprehensive territorial systems, on the other hand, is far more complicated, and locating the toponyms recorded in a particular list is only the first step in that enterprise. Several other factors have to be considered, namely the historical, functional, historiographical and ideological. The combination of all these aspects involves so many uncertainties that it is hardly surprising that opinions about the historicity, date, function and ideological background of the geographical lists are so divergent.

Years of studying these problems have convinced me that much still remains to be done in investigating and interpreting the lists, and that they still conceal a great deal of information that may in due course provide answers to the many questions that remain to be solved.

The seven studies in this book are the result of a decade of teaching advanced students at Tel Aviv University. Some of the ideas presented here have been shared with those students, from whom I learned a great deal and whose stimulating comments and papers helped me to formulate my thoughts. I hope that this work will encourage other scholars to advance the investigation of the lists, which are a most important source for the history of Israel in the time of the Monarchy.

The study of historical geography is extremely complicated, due to the abundance of topographical, archaeological, historical and literary factors that have to be considered. In this book, certain subjects have been dealt with in more than one chapter, calling for constant cross-reference.

The biblical quotations follow the Revised Standard Version, except where, as indicated, my own translation differs from it. Hebrew words and names are transcribed in italics; the spelling of biblical names follows that of the Revised Standard Version. A differentiation has been made between Hebrew and Arabic spellings, e.g., 'Tel' and 'Tell'. For technical reasons, phonetic signs had to be inserted by hand; the German Umlaut is represented by 'e'; accents have sometimes been omitted. The maps are a-historical in that they include both modern and old names.

The completed manuscript of this book was handed to the publisher in October 1983. Therefore no publications after this date are referred to either in the text or in the bibliographical notes.

Finally, I should like to express gratitude to all those who have encouraged and helped me to produce this book. First and foremost my thanks are due to my friend Ora Lipschitz for suggesting this study for inclusion in the Jerusalem Biblical Studies, for all the time she spent editing the various drafts of the work, and for her invaluable suggestions at every stage; to my colleague Professor I. Eph'al for his comments and corrections, and his care in eliminating inconsistencies; to Professor A. Rofé for improving the manuscript with his suggestions; to the publishers, Simor, for accepting the book and seeing it through in spite of all difficulties; to Ruth Connell Robertson for her active involvement in the project, especially with regard to its English style; to Judith Dekel and Ora Paran of the Institute of Archaeology at Tel Aviv University for preparing the maps; and to S. Friedman for compiling the indexes and assisting with the maps.

Any errors that remain in the finished product are entirely mine, as are the opinions expressed in these seven studies.

Jerusalem, 1986 N.N.

ABBREVIATIONS

I BIBLIOGRAPHICAL ABBREVIATIONS

A basic bibliography for each chapter is provided in the relevant footnotes.

Abel, *Geographie*	F. M. Abel, *Geographie de la Palestine,* vol. 2 (Paris 1938).
Abel, "Tappouah"	F. M. Abel, "Tappouah", *Revue Biblique,* vol. 45 (1936), pp. 103-112.
Aharoni, *LB*	Y. Aharoni, *The Land of the Bible: A Historical Geography* (London and Philadelphia 1967). [The pagination in the following is of this first edition. The revised edition published in 1979 is paginated differently].
Aharoni, "Remarks"	Y. Aharoni, "Some Geographical Remarks concerning the Campaigns of Amenhotep II", *JNES,* vol. 19 (1960), pp. 177-183.
Aharoni, *Settlement*	Y. Aharoni, *The Settlement of the Israelite Tribes in Upper Galilee* (Jerusalem 1957) [Hebrew].
Aharoni, "Solomonic"	Y. Aharoni, "The Solomonic Districts", *Tel Aviv,* vol. 3 (1976), pp. 5-15.
Albright, *Religion*	W.F. Albright, *Archaeology and the Religion of Israel* (Baltimore 1942).
Albright, "Divisions"	W.F. Albright, "The Administrative Divisions of Israel and Judah", *JPOS,* vol. 5 (1925), pp. 17-54.

Albright "Issachar"	W.F. Albright, "The Topography of the Tribe of Issachar", *ZAW*, vol. 44 (1926), pp. 225-236.
Albright "Levitic"	W.F. Albright, "The List of Levitic Cities", in: *Louis Ginzberg Jubilee Volume* (New York 1945), pp. 49-73.
Alt, "Galilaeische Ortsliste"	A. Alt, "Eine galilaeische Ortsliste in Jos. 19", *ZAW*, vol. 45 (1927), pp. 59-81.
Alt, "Israels Gaue"	A. Alt, "Israels Gaue unter Salomo", *Alttestamentliche Studien Rudolf Kittel zum 60. Geburtstag dargebracht*, (Leipzig 1913), pp. 1-19. Reprint *KS*, vol. 2 (1953), pp. 76-89.
Alt, "Judaeische Ortslisten"	A. Alt, "Bemerkungen zu einigen judaeischen Ortslisten des Alten Testaments", *Beitraege zur biblischen Landes- und Altertumskunde*, vol. 68 (1951), pp. 193-210. Reprint *KS*, vol. 2 (1953), pp. 289-305.
Alt, "Judas Gaue"	A. Alt, "Judas Gaue unter Josia", *Palaestinajahrbuch*, vol. 21 (1925), pp. 100-116. Reprint *KS*, vol. 2 (1953), pp. 276-288.
Alt, "Landnahme"	A. Alt, "Die Landnahme der Israeliten in Palaestina", *Reformationsprogramm der Universitaet Leipzig* (1925). Reprint *KS*, vol. 1 (1953), pp. 89-125.
Alt, "Provinzen"	A. Alt, "Das System der assyrischen Provinzen auf dem Boden des Reiches Israel", *ZDPV*, vol. 52 (1929), pp. 220-242. Reprint *KS*, vol. 2 (1953), pp. 188-205.

Alt, "Staatenbildung"	A. Alt, "Die Staatenbildung der Israeliten in Palaestina", *Reformationsprogramm der Universitaet Leipzig* (1930). Reprint *KS*, vol. 2 (1953), pp. 1-65.
Alt, "Stadtstaat"	A. Alt, "Der Stadtstaat Samaria", *Berichte ueber die Verhandlungen der Saechsischen Akademie der Wissenschaften zu Leipzig*, Phil. -hist. Klasse, Band 101 Heft 5 (Berlin 1954). Reprint *KS*, vol. 3 (1959), pp. 258-302.
Alt, "System"	A. Alt, "Das System der Stammesgrenzen im Buche Josua", *Sellin-Festschrift. Beitraege zur Religionsgeschichte und Archaeologie Palaestinas* (Leipzig 1927), pp. 13-24. Reprint *KS*, vol. 1 (1953), pp. 193-202.
Auld, "Levitical"	A. G. Auld, "The 'Levitical Cities': Texts and History", *ZAW*, vol. 91 (1979), pp. 194-206.
Avi-Yonah, *Gazetteer*	M. Avi-Yonah, *Gazetteer of Roman Palestine*, Qedem, vol. 5 (Jerusalem 1976).
Baechli, "Liste"	O. Baechli, "Von der Liste zur Beschreibung: Beobachtungen und Erwaegungen zu Jos. 13-19", *ZDPV*, vol. 89 (1973), pp. 1-14.
Boree, *Ortsnamen*	W. Boree, *Die Alten Ortsnamen Palaestinas* (Leipzig 1930).
Cooke, *Joshua*	G. A. Cooke, *The Book of Joshua, The Cambridge Bible for Schools and Colleges* (Cambridge 1918).

Cross-Wright "Boundary"	F. M. Cross & G. E. Wright, "The Boundary and Province Lists of the Kingdom of Judah", *JBL,* vol. 75 (1956), pp. 202-226.
Cruesemann, *Widerstand*	F. Cruesemann, *Der Widerstand gegen das Koenigtum: Die antikoeniglichen Texte des Alten Testaments und der Kampf um den fruehen israelitischen Staat,* Wissenschaftliche Monographien zum Alten und Neuen Testament, vol. 49 (Neukirchen-Vluyn 1978).
Driver, *Samuel*	S.R. Driver, *Notes on the Hebrew Text and the Topography of the Books of Samuel* (Oxford 1913).
Edel, "Stelen"	E. Edel, "Die Stelen Amenophis' II aus Karnak und Memphis mit dem Bericht ueber die asiatischen Feldzuege des Koenigs", *ZDPV,* vol. 69 (1953), pp. 97-176.
Elliger, "Grenze"	K. Elliger, "Die Grenze zwischen Ephraim und Manasse", *ZDPV,* vol. 53 (1930), pp. 265-309.
Elliger, "Michmethath"	K. Elliger, "Michmethath", in: *Archaeologie und Altes Testament. Festschrift fuer Kurt Galling,* eds. A. Kuschke and E. Kutsch (Tuebingen 1970), pp. 91-100.
Elliger, "Neues"	K. Elliger, "Neues ueber die Grenze zwischen Ephraim und Manasse", *JPOS,* vol. 18 (1938), pp. 7-16.
Eusebius, *Onomastikon*	Eusebius, *Das Onomastikon der biblischen Ortsnamen,* ed. E. Klostermann (Leipzig 1904; Reprint Hildesheim 1966).
Forrer, *Provinz*	E. Forrer, *Die Provinzeinteilung des assyrischen Reiches* (Leipzig 1920).

Gal, *Issachar*	Z. Gal, *Ramat Issachar: Ancient Settlements in a Peripheral Region* (Tel Aviv 1980) [Hebrew].
Gal, "Tel Rekhesh"	Z. Gal, "Tel Rekhesh and Tel Qarnei Hittin", *Eretz Israel,* vol. 15 (1981), pp. 213-221 [Hebrew].
Gardiner, "Road"	A. H. Gardiner, "The Ancient Military Road between Egypt and Palestine", *JEA,* vol. 6 (1920), pp. 99-116.
de Geus, *Tribes*	C. H. J. de Geus, *The Tribes of Israel: An Investigation into some of the Presuppositions of M. Noth Amphictyony Hypothesis,* Studia Semitica Neerlandica, vol. 18 (Assen-Amsterdam 1976).
Gottwald, *Tribes*	N. K. Gottwald, *The Tribes of Yahweh: A Sociology of the Religion of Liberated Israel 1250-1050 B.C.E.* (New York 1979).
Haran, "Studies"	M. Haran, "Studies in the Account of the Levitical Cities", *JBL,* vol. 80 (1961), pp. 45-54, 156-165.
Haran, *Temples*	M. Haran, *Temples and Temple-Service in Ancient Israel: An Inquiry into the Character of Cult Phenomena and the Historical Setting of the Priestly School* (Oxford 1978).
Helck, *Beziehungen*	W. Helck, *Die Beziehungen Aegyptens zu Vorderasien im 3. und 2. Jahrtausend v. Chr.* Second edition (Wiesbaden, 1971).
Herrmann, "Issakar"	W. Herrmann, "Issakar", *Forschungen und Fortschritte,* vol. 37 (1963), pp. 21-26.

Ishida, *Studies*	T. Ishida (ed.), *Studies in the Period of David and Solomon* (Tokyo 1982).
Jenni, "Grenze"	E. Jenni, "Historisch-topographische Untersuchungen zur Grenze zwischen Ephraim und Manasse", *ZDPV,* vol. 74 (1958), pp. 35-40.
Kallai, "Boundaries"	Z. Kallai, "The Boundaries of Canaan and the Land of Israel in the Bible", *Eretz Israel,* vol. 12 (1975), pp. 27-34 [Hebrew].
Kallai, "Frameworks"	Z. Kallai, "Organizational and Administrative Frameworks in the Kingdom of David and Solomon", *Proceedings of the Sixth World Congress of Jewish Studies,* vol. 1 (Jerusalem 1977), pp. 213-220.
Kallai, "System"	Z. Kallai, "The System of Levitic Cities - A Historical-Geographical Study in Biblical Historiography", *Zion,* vol. 45 (1980), pp. 13-34 [Hebrew].
Kallai, "Town Lists"	Z. Kallai-Kleinmann, "The Town Lists of Judah, Simeon, Benjamin and Dan", *VT,* vol. 8 (1958), pp. 134-160.
Kallai, *Tribes*	Z. Kallai, *The Tribes of Israel: A Study in the Historical Geography of the Bible* (Jerusalem 1967) [Hebrew].
Kallai, "United Monarchy"	Z. Kallai, "The United Monarchy of Israel - A Focal Point in Israelite Historiography", *IEJ* vol. 27 (1977), pp. 103-109.
Klein, *Galilee*	S. Klein, *Galilee. Geography and History of Galilee from the Return from Babylonia to the Conclusion of the Talmud* (Jerusalem 1945; second edition 1967) [Hebrew].

Kochavi, *Judaea*	M. Kochavi (ed.), *Judaea, Samaria and the Golan. Archaeological Survey 1967-1968* (Jerusalem 1972) [Hebrew].
Kuschke, "Beitraege"	A. Kuschke, "Historisch-topographische Beitraege zum Buche Josua", in: *Gottes Wort und Gottes Land. Festschrift fuer H. W. Hertzberg, ed. G. Reventlow* (Goettingen 1965), pp. 90-109.
Lemaire, "Bene Jacob"	A. Lemaire, "Les Bene Jacob:Essai d'Interpretation Historique d'une Tradition Patriarcale", *RB,* vol. 85 (1978), pp. 321-337.
Lemaire, "Hepher"	A. Lemaire, "Le 'pays de Hepher' et les 'filles de Zelophehad' a la lumiere des ostraca de Samarie", *Semitica,* vol. 22 (1972), pp. 13-20.
Lemaire, *Inscriptions*	A. Lemaire, *Inscriptions hebraiques,* vol. I: Les Ostraca (Paris 1977).
Mazar, "Dan"	B. Mazar, "The Cities of the Territory of Dan", *IEJ,* vol. 10 (1960), pp. 65-77.
Mazar, *Judges*	B. Mazar (ed.), *Judges,* in: *The World History of the Jewish People,* First series: Ancient Times, vol. 3 Jerusalem 1971.
Mazar, "Lebo"	B. Maisler (Mazar), "Lebo-hamath and the Northern Boundary of Canaan", *BJPES,* vol. 12 (1946), pp. 91-102 Reprint in: *Cities and Districts in Eretz Israel* (Jerusalem 1975), pp. 167-181 [Hebrew].

Mazar, "Levites"	B. Mazar, "The Cities of the Priests and the Levites", *SVT,* vol. 7 (1960), pp. 193-205.
Mazar, "Sanctuary"	B. Mazar, "The Sanctuary of Arad and the Family of Hobab the Kenite", *JNES,* vol. 24 (1965), pp. 297-303.
Mettinger, *Officials*	T. N. D. Mettinger, *Solomonic State Officials: A Study of the Civil Government Officials of the Israelite Monarchy.* Coniectanea Biblica Old Testament Series, vol. 5 (Lund 1971).
Montgomery, *Kings*	J. A. Montgomery, *The Books of Kings, ICC* (Edinburgh 1951).
Mowinckel, *Quellen*	S. Mowinckel, *Zur Frage nach dokumentarischen Quellen in Josua 13 - 19* (Oslo 1946).
Mowinckel, *Tetrateuch*	S. Mowinckel, *Tetrateuch - Pentateuch - Hexateuch: Die Berichte ueber die Landnahme in den drei altisraelitischen Geschichtswerken,* BZAW, vol. 90 (Berlin 1964).
Na'aman, "Amarna"	N. Na'aman, "The Political Disposition and Historical Development of Eretz-Israel according to the Amarna Letters", PhD Thesis (Tel Aviv 1975).
Na'aman, "Brook"	N. Na'aman, "The Brook of Egypt and Assyrian Policy on the Border of Egypt", *Tel Aviv,* vol. 6 (1979), pp. 68-90.
Na'aman, "Shihor"	N. Na'aman, "The Shihor of Egypt and Shur that is before Egypt", *Tel Aviv,* vol. 7 (1980), pp. 95-109.

Na'aman, "Simeon"	N. Na'aman, "The Inheritance of the Sons of Simeon", *ZDPV*, vol. 96 (1980), pp. 136-152.
Noth, *History*	M. Noth, *The History of Israel* (second edition, London 1958; translated by S. Godman from the second German edition of 1954).
Noth, *Josua*	M. Noth, *Das Buch Josua, Handbuch zum Alten Testament*, vol. I,7, second edition (Tuebingen 1953).
Noth, "Studien"	M. Noth, "Studien zu den historisch-geographischen Dokumenten des Josuabuches", *ZDPV*, vol. 58 (1935), pp. 185-255. Reprint in: *Aufsaetze zur biblischen Landes- und Altertumskunde*, vol. 1 (Neukirchen-Vluyn 1971), pp. 229-280.
Noth, "Thappuah"	M. Noth, "Thappuah und Jasub", *ZDPV*, vol. 82 (1966), pp. 270-273.
Noth, "Ueberlieferung"	M. Noth, "Ueberlieferungsgeschichtliches zur zweiten Haelfte des Josuabuches", in: *Alttestamentliche Studien, Friedrich Noetscher zum 60 Geburtstag Gewidmet*, Bonner Biblische Beitraege, vol. 1 (Bonn 1950), pp. 152-167.
Otto, *Jakob*	E. Otto, *Jakob in Sichem: Ueberlieferungsgeschichtliche, archaeologische und territorialgeschichtliche Studien zur Entstehungsgeschichte Israels*, BWANT vol. 110 (Stuttgart 1979).
Pintore, "Intendenti"	F. Pintore, "I dodici intendenti di Salomone", *RSO*, vol. 45 (1970), pp. 177-207.

Roesel, "Kriege"	H. Roesel, "Studien zur Topographie der Kriege in den Buechern Josua und Richter", *ZDPV*, vol. 91 (1975), pp. 159-190; vol. 92 (1976), pp. 10-46.
Saarisalo, *Boundary*	A. Saarisalo, *The Boundary between Issachar and Naphtali: An Archaeological and Literary Study of Israel's Settlement in Canaan.* Annales Academiae scientiarum Fennicae, Ser. B XXI,3 (Helsinki 1927).
Saebo, "Landideal"	M. Saebo, "Grenzbeschreibung und Landideal im Alten Testament mit besonderer Beruecksichtigung der min-'ad Formel", *ZDPV*, vol. 90 (1974), pp. 14-37.
Schmitt, "Bet-awen"	G. Schmitt, "Bet-Awen", in: R. Cohen und G. Schmitt, *Drei Studien zur Archaeologie und Topographie Altisraels*, Beihefte TAVO, Reihe B Nr. 44 (Wiesbaden 1980), pp. 33-76.
Schmitt, *Frieden*	G. Schmitt, *Du sollst keinen Frieden schliessen mit den Bewohnern des Landes: Die Weisungen gegen die Kanaanaeer in Israels Geschichte und Geschichtsschreibung*, BWANT, vol. 91 (Stuttgart 1970).
Schmitt, "Gat"	G. Schmitt, "Gat, Gittaim und Gitta", in: R. Cohen und G. Schmitt, *Drei Studien zur Archaeologie und Topographie Altisraels*, Beihefte TAVO, Reihe B Nr. 44 (Wiesbaden 1980), pp. 77-138.
Simons, *Geographical*	J. Simons, *The Geographical and Topographical Texts of the Old Testament* (Leiden 1959).

Simons, "Structure"	J. Simons, "The Structure and Interpretation of Josh. XVI-XVII", in: *Orientalia Neerlandica. A Volume of Oriental Studies* (Leiden 1948), pp. 190-215.
Steuernagel, *Josua*	C. Steuernagel, *Uebersetzung und Erklaerung der Buecher Deuteronomium und Josua und allgemeine Einleitung in den Hexateuch, Goettinger Handkommentar zum AT,* vol. I,3 (Goettingen 1900).
Strange, "Dan"	J. Strange, "The Inheritance of Dan", *Studia Theologica,* vol. 20 (1966), pp. 120-139.
Strecker, *Das Land*	G. Strecker (ed.), *Das Land Israel in biblischer Zeit: Jerusalem Symposium 1981,* Goettinger Theologische Arbeiten vol. 25 (Goettingen 1983).
Taeubler, *Biblische Studien*	E. Taeubler, *Biblische Studien: Die Epoche der Richter,* ed. H. J. Zobel (Tuebingen 1958).
de Vaux, *Ancient Israel*	R. de Vaux, *Ancient Israel its Life and Institutions* (London 1961; translated by J. McHuge from the original French edition of 1958, 1960).
de Vaux, *Early History*	R. de Vaux, *The Early History of Israel* (London 1978; translated from the French edition of 1971).
Wallis, "Thaanath-silo"	G. Wallis, "Thaanath-Silo", *ZDPV,* vol. 77 (1961), pp. 38-45.
Weippert, *Settlement*	M. Weippert, *The Settlement of the Israelite Tribes in Palestine: A Critical Survey of Recent Scholarly Debate,* Studies in Biblical Theology, second series vol. 21 (London 1971; translated from the German edition of 1967).

Wright, "Provinces"	G. E. Wright, "The Provinces of Solomon (1 Kings 4:7-19), *Eretz Israel,* vol. 8 (1967), pp. 58*-68*.
Wuest, *Untersuchungen*	M. Wuest, *Untersuchungen zu den siedlungs-geographischen Texten des Alten Testaments,* Teil 1: Ostjordanland, Beihefte TAVO, Reihe B Nr. 9 (Wiesbaden 1975).
Zoebel, "Abel-mehola"	H. J. Zoebel, "Abel-Mehola", *ZDPV,* vol. 82 (1966), pp. 83-108.

II OTHER ABBREVIATIONS

AASOR	Annual of the American Schools of Oriental Research, New Haven.
ANET	Ancient Near Eastern Texts relating to the Old Testament, ed. by J.B. Pritchard, second edition (Princeton 1955).
AOAT	Alter Orient und Altes Testament, Neukirchen-Vluyn.
AT	Altes Testament.
ATD	Das Alte Testament Deutsch, Goettingen.
BASOR	Bulletin of the American Schools of Oriental Research, New Haven.
BIES	Bulletin of the Israel Exploration Society, Jerusalem.
BJPES	Bulletin of the Jewish Palestine Exploration Society, Jerusalem.
BK	Biblischer Kommentar, Neukirchen-Vluyn.
BWANT	Beitraege zur Wissenschaft vom Alten und Neuen Testament, (Leipzig) Stuttgart.
BZAW	Beihefte zur Zeitschrift fuer die Alttestamentliche Wissenschaft, (Giessen) Berlin.

CBQ	Catholic Biblical Quarterly, Washington D.C.
EA	El Amarna.
EAEHL	Encyclopaedia of Archaeological Excavations in the Holy Land, ed. M. Avi-Yonah, Jerusalem.
EM	Encyclopaedia Miqra'it (Encyclopaedia Biblica), Jerusalem [Hebrew].
Eretz Israel	Archaeological, Historical and Geographical Studies, Jerusalem [Hebrew].
HThR	Harvard Theological Review, Cambridge, Mass.
ICC	The International Critical Commentary, Edinburgh.
IEJ	Israel Exploration Journal, Jerusalem.
JAOS	Journal of the American Oriental Society (Boston), New Haven.
JBL	Journal of Biblical Literature, (New York, New Haven) Philadelphia.
JEA	Journal of Egyptian Archaeology, London.
JNES	Journal of Near Eastern Studies, Chicago.
JPOS	Journal of the Palestine Oriental Society, Jerusalem.
JQR	Jewish Quarterly Review, Philadelphia.
JSOT	Journal for the Study of the Old Testament, Sheffield.
K	Ketib
KS	Kleine Schriften [see Alt, p. 16 above].
LB	Land of the Bible [see Aharoni p. 15 above].
LXX	Septuagint
MSS	Manuscripts.
MT	Massoretic Text
PEF QSt	Palestine Exploration Fund. Quarterly Statement, London.
PEQ	Palestine Exploration Quarterly, London.
PJb	Palaestinajahrbuch, Berlin.
Q	Qere

Qadmoniot	Quarterly for the Antiquities of Eretz-Israel and Bible Lands, Jerusalem.
Qedem	Monographs of the Institute of Archaeology, The Hebrew University, Jerusalem.
RB	Revue Biblique, Paris.
RSO	Rivista degli Studi Orientali, Roma.
RSV	Revised Standard Version.
Scripta Hierosolymitana	Publications of the Hebrew University, Jerusalem.
Shnaton	An Annual for Biblical and Ancient Near Eastern Studies, Jerusalem / Tel Aviv.
SVT	Supplements to Vetus Testamentum, Leiden.
Tarbiz	A Quarterly for Jewish Studies, Jerusalem.
TAVO	Tuebinger Atlas des Vorderen Orients, Wiesbaden.
Tel Aviv	Journal of the Tel Aviv University Institute for Archaeology, Tel Aviv.
ThLZ	Theologische Literaturzeitung, Leipzig / Berlin.
VT	Vetus Testamentum, Leiden.
ZAW	Zeitschrift fuer die Alttestamentliche Wissenschaft, (Giessen) Berlin.
ZDPV	Zeitschrift des Deutschen Palaestina-Vereins (Leipzig, Stuttgart), Wiesbaden.
Zion	A Quarterly for Research in Jewish History, Jerusalem.

INTRODUCTION

The geographical lists in the Bible are of major importance in studying the historical geography of the Land of Canaan in the biblical period. They were drawn up for various purposes and their present context may differ substantially from the one for which they were originally intended. Therefore both the facts included in the lists and their historical significance have been matters of controversy.

The Bible contains four major 'systems' covering extensive territory on both sides of the Jordan:

(1) The Land of Canaan (Num. 34; Ezek. 47).

(2) The boundary system of the Israelite tribes (Josh. 13-19).

(3) The list of Levitical cities (Josh. 21; 1 Chr. 6:54-81 [=MT 6:39-66]).

(4) The list of Solomon's districts (1 Kings 4:7-19).

Other lists, directly related to these comprehensive territorial systems and forming an integral part of this study, are to be found in the books of Joshua and Judges:

(5) The list of unconquered Canaanite cities (Judg. 1:21, 27-35).

(6) "The land that yet remains" (Josh. 13:2-6).

(7) The six cities of refuge (Josh. 20:7-9).

Each of the studies in this book attempts to clarify some of the topographical and historical aspects of the systems. It is also hoped to further the understanding of the geographical lists by demonstrating how they were used by biblical historiographers, and by trying to establish the relationship between the lists and the administration of the Age of the Monarchy.

Modern research on the territorial systems was initiated by the eminent scholar A. Alt, who, in a series of brilliant articles mostly published in the 1920s, both analysed the systems themselves and established the basic principles for the study of the geographical lists.[1] They are so important for any study of historical geography that they are briefly sketched here.

(a) Since administrative systems are always established according to the topography of the land, they last for a very long time. Even changes of regime or population hardly ever result in any but the most minor alterations in territorial divisions. Therefore, in order to understand properly the territorial divisions of any country, one should investigate as extensive a period as possible.

1. Alt, "Israels Gaue"; id., "Landnahme"; id., "Judas Gaue"; id., "System"; id., "Galilaeische Ortsliste".

(b) The way to obtain absolute dates for the various systems is first to establish a relative chronology by comparing the lists with one another; then to take those lists which have a firm date (e.g., the Solomonic district system) as a reference point for dating all other lists. Alt held that it is thus possible to establish the history of the territorial divisions in the country and the changes that occurred in its borders.

(c) Study of the lists should be independent of the documentary hypothesis, since they may have had a life of their own prior to their incorporation in the historiographic books of the Bible. Therefore the date and composition of each geographical list should be determined by analysing the text, structure and content of the list itself, and not by assigning it to its present setting in, or relating to, one of the documents.

(d) The geographical lists should be classified on the basis of literary criteria. Thus, in analysing the tribal allotments in Josh. 13-19, Alt separated the boundary delineations from the town lists. His view that the boundary descriptions are of an early date and that the town lists belong to the administrative system of the Divided Monarchy is now generally accepted.

Today it is taken for granted that archaeology is the cornerstone of any study of the historical geography of the biblical period. The credit for this undoubtedly goes to

W.F. Albright, who initiated this type of investigation.[2] By a careful examination of the results of excavations, he was able to redate the levels of occupation at various sites and to demonstrate the close connection between them and the geographical lists.

In recent years, extensive archaeological research on both sides of the Jordan has provided a vast quantity of data, both from excavations with precisely-dated occupational levels and from wide area surveys. The present writer has tried to make use of the most up-to-date data available, but the immense accumulation of material presents a real challenge for future researchers.

Since the foundations of historical geography were laid by Alt and Albright, many studies have been published, and an attempt has been made here to include as many bibliographical references as possible in the footnotes. An extensive history of research was undertaken by Z. Kallai in his

2. The following is a partial list of Albright's early articles of the 1920s: "Contributions to the Historical Geography of Palestine", *AASOR*, vols. 2-3 (1923), pp. 1-46; "Researches of the School in Western Judaea", *BASOR*, no. 15 (1924), pp. 2-11; Excavations and Results at Tell el-Ful (Gibeah of Saul), *AASOR*, vol. 4 (1924), pp. 90-160; "Egypt and the Early History of the Negeb", *JPOS*, vol. 4 (1924), pp. 131-161; "Divisions"; "Issachar"; "The Jordan Valley in the Bronze Age", *AASOR*, vol. 6 (1926), pp. 13-74; "The Site of Tirzah and the Topography of Western Manasseh", *JPOS*, vol. 11 (1931), pp. 241-251.

extremely detailed work.[3] This book is undoubtedly the most thorough treatment of the subject. It discusses the delineation of the boundaries, clarifies the date and scope of various territorial systems, and compares the systems with each other. Kallai's exhaustive work has greatly advanced our understanding of the divisions of the country, especially the tribal allotments. It is therefore only natural that in our study, Kallai is taken as a point of departure.

Of the four systems mentioned above, only the fourth, the list of Solomon's officials, appears in the Bible as an administrative document. The other three are now embodied in different contexts, and there is no evidence that they ever played a role in the administration during the biblical period.

Some scholars regarded the lists as unrealistic, dating their composition either to the beginning of the history of Israel,[4] or to the post-exilic period.[5] This interpretation was

3. Kallai, *Tribes*, pp. 2-13; cf. de Vaux, *Early History*, pp. 727-731.

4. Y. Kaufmann, *History of the Religion of Israel*, part 4 (Jerusalem 1947), pp. 377-393 [Hebrew]; id., *The Biblical Account of the Conquest of Palestine*, translated from the Hebrew by M. Dagut (Jerusalem 1953), *passim*.

5. For the post-exilic date of the entire Priestly Code and therefore also the lists, see J. Wellhausen, Die Composition des Hexateuchs und der Historischen Buecher des AT, fourth edition (Berlin 1963), pp. 116-134; J.G. Vink, "The Date and Origin of the Priestly Code in the Old Testament", *Oudtestamentische Studien*, vol. 15

based on literary and ideological considerations and not on careful analysis of the topographical information contained in the lists. Other scholars rejected this approach, regarding the lists as administrative documents reflecting an actual situation within a particular period. They pointed to the historicity of many details in the lists, located the toponyms, and delineated the borders. Their conclusion was that entire lists were authentic documents from which the historical situation could legitimately be reconstructed.

This latter attitude has found broad acceptance, but there is another possible interpretation which has not yet been properly examined: that the writers who composed these descriptions combined two types of elements, the actual and the ideal, or one might say the historical and hypothetical. Even if one part of a list reflects an actual situation, the

(1969), pp. 1-144. This line of enquiry was further developed by Mowinckel, *Quellen;* id., *Tetrateuch,* pp. 51-78. In his opinion, the entire section in the book of Joshua describing the inheritances of the tribes (Josh. 13-19) was first composed by a Priestly writer after the exile. This writer was obliged to describe the boundary system from oral traditions, since no written documents survived after the fall of Jerusalem. The tradition represents the state of knowledge in the time of the late Priestly writer, reflecting a mixture of many historical situations from the time of the Judges until the last days of the Kingdom of Judah. The varied nature of the descriptions in Josh. 13-19 is explained by the multiplicity of historical situations and administrative structures contained in the boundary system.

historicity of the entire system does not necessarily follow. The writers could have used an authentic document as a core and built a complete system around it. In other words, some components of the system might be literary creations. In that case, the entire system must be regarded as artificial, even though its kernel, or a substantial part of it is authentic.

Another factor that has to be considered when trying to understand the systems is the possible bias of the men who composed the accounts. Many of the writers were undoubtedly men of Judaean origin who would have tried to recount events in a light favourable to their own tribe and kingdom. This bias becomes very obvious when these writers describe the Northern Kingdom, and is also evident elsewhere in the Bible. It is important to note that such geographical lists are included in compositions with a definite historiographical purpose - to describe the occupation of the land by the tribes of Israel. One must therefore consider the extent to which the origin of the writers may have influenced their treatment of the border delineations. Did they, as many scholars believe, simply copy the original documents verbatim? Or did they alter the facts in favour of their tribe, in order to glorify its past and improve its image?

There is a further aspect that has to be taken into account. The many ancient documents unearthed all over Hither Asia have enabled scholars to reconstruct the administrations of many of the kingdoms of the ancient Near East. These can serve as patterns with which the biblical system may be compared. The administration of neighbouring kingdoms is of major importance in our attempt to reconstruct the organization and administration of the Age of the Monarchy, because biblical writers did not record this kind of data systematically, and only rarely mentioned any details at all. On the other hand, it must be borne in mind that our present knowledge of the administration of Israel's immediate neighbours (e.g., Aram, Moab, Ammon, Tyre, Sidon) is minimal, and one could scarcely expect to find a close resemblance between the Israelite administration and that of distant Near Eastern kingdoms (e.g., Egypt, Assyria, Babylonia). Therefore the documents of the ancient Near East can do no more than provide a general model to help determine the feasibility of various interpretations.

CHAPTER ONE

THE BORDERS OF THE TRIBES OF ISRAEL WEST OF THE JORDAN AND "THE LAND THAT YET REMAINS"

1) Introduction

In an article published in 1980 I wrote: "...the Old Testament contains three basic territorial concepts, each with its own set of borders: (a) the Land of Canaan, which was adopted from the local inhabitants at the time that the Israelites first settled... (b) the kingdom of David and Solomon, excluding the vassal states, reflected by the borders of the tribes of Israel... (c) the kingdom promised by the Deuteronomist for the end of days, which embodied the 'Patriarchs' borders' and envisioned the Israelite nation extending over all the territory of 'Beyond the River' from the Nile to the Euphrates".[1] The 'Patriarchs' borders' were never described in detail and do not belong to the same category as the other two. These - the borders of the Land of Canaan (Num. 34; Ezek. 47) and of the tribes of Israel (the boundary system, Josh. 13-19) - were described in great detail and can be accurately delineated.

The territorial gap between these two sets of borders, designated in the Bible as "the land that yet remains" (Josh. 13:2-6), is the subject of this chapter. The demarcation of the

1. Na'aman, "Shihor", p. 98.

'remaining land' and its precise relationship to the borders, as well as the historical significance of the territorial concepts embodied in the borders of the Land of Canaan and the boundary system, are still controversial.[2] It is the purpose of this chapter to delineate the boundaries of the tribes of Israel west of the Jordan and the remaining land in both the north and the south, and to place them in their appropriate historical context.

2) The Inheritances of Naphtali and Asher and the Northern Border of "the Land that Yet Remains"

The northern border of the tribes of Israel could ostensibly be deduced from the account of the inheritances of the tribes of Asher and Naphtali in Josh. 19. However, even a cursory examination shows that the demarcation is not simple. The

2. For previous discussions of the boundaries of the remaining land and the tribes of Israel west of the Jordan, see F. Buhl, "Textkritische Bemerkungen zu Jos. 13:4-5", *Mitteilungen und Nachrichten des Deutschen Palaestina Vereins,* vol. 1 (1895), pp. 53-55; Alt, "Galilaeische Ortsliste" p. 69; B. Maisler [=Mazar], *Untersuchungen zur alten Geschichte und Ethnographie Syriens und Palaestinas* (Giessen 1930), pp. 59-67; Noth, "Studien", pp. 222-223, 227-228; id., *Josua, passim;* D. Baldi, "La Terra Promessa nel Programma di Giosue", *Studii Biblici Franciscani Liber Annuus,* vol. 1 (1950/1951), pp. 87-106; Aharoni, *Settlement,* pp. 76-89; id., *LB, passim;* id., *The Inheritance of Asher between Misrephoth-maim and Shihor-libnath* (Sulam Zor and Ga'aton Councils 1970) [Brochure, Hebrew]; Simons, *Geographical,* pp. 109-113; Kallai, *Tribes, passim;* id., "Boundaries"; Saebo, "Landideal".

northern border of Naphtali is missing altogether (Josh. 19:32-34), and despite its detailed description, the northern border of Asher (Josh. 19:28-29) is far from clear. Numerous questions immediately pose themselves: Why was the northern border of Naphtali ignored (or omitted) by the writer? Where should this border be drawn? What is the territorial meaning of the term "Sidon the Great" (Josh. 19:28)? How can the repetition of the verb *šwb* (turns) in the northern border of Asher be explained? Why was that border of Asher described in such detail?

As a starting-point for an inquiry into these questions one may take the similarity of the descriptions as they appear in several biblical sources relating to the tribal borders (Josh. 11:3, 8, 17; 12:7; 13:4-6; Judg. 3:3; 2 Sam. 24:5-7). Combining some of these passages may help to resolve our queries.

	Josh. 13:4-6	Josh. 11:8	Judg. 3:3
(4)	...all the land of the	And the Lord gave them	...and all the
	Canaanites,	into the hand of Israel,	Canaanites,
	and Mearah which belongs	who smote them and	and the
	to the Sidonians,	chased them as far as	Sidonians,
	to Aphek, to the boundary	Great Sidon	
	of the Amorites, (5a) and		
	the land of the Gebalites,		
(6)	all the inhabitants of		
	the hill country		and the Hivites
	from Lebanon to	and	who dwelt on
	Misrephoth-maim...	Misrephoth-maim,	
(5b)	and all Lebanon, toward		Mount Lebanon,
	the sunrising, from Baal-gad		from Mount Baal-
	below Mount Hermon to	and eastward as far as	hermon as far as
	the entrance of Hamath.	the valley of Mizpeh...	the entrance of Hamath.

In order to demonstrate the uniformity of the territorial concept in all three passages, verses 5 and 6 in Josh. 13 have been transposed.

a) Baal-gad Below Mount Hermon (Josh. 13:5)

Baal-gad appears in two juxtapositions (from...to...): on the one hand it is the opposite extremity of Lebo-hamath (Josh. 13:5), on the other hand of mount Halak (Josh. 11:17; 12:7). Lebo-hamath marks the northern border of Canaan (Num. 34:8) and mount Halak the south-eastern border of the tribal allotments. Baal-gad must therefore be located on the northern border of the tribal allotments, which is the southern border of the remaining land.

To gain a better topographical understanding of Josh. 13:5 it must be noted that here "...all Lebanon, toward the sunrising..." as well as the picturesque "... a tower of Lebanon, overlooking Damascus" (Cant. 7:4) refer to the Anti-Lebanon mountain range. The southern peak of this range (Jebel esh-Sheikh) is usually called Hermon in the Bible (e.g., Deut. 3:8; 4:48; Josh. 12:1, 5; Judg. 3:3; 1 Chr. 5:23).[3]

Baal-gad is also described as "in the valley of Lebanon" (Josh. 11:17; 12:7). The valley of Lebanon is certainly to be identified with the Beqa' in Lebanon, which is north-west of

3. Y. Ikeda, "Hermon, Sirion and Senir", *Annual of the Japanese Biblical Institute*, vol. 4 (1978), pp. 32, 37.

mount Hermon. Thus there seems to be a discrepancy between the description of Baal-gad as being "below Mount Hermon" (Josh. 13:5) and "in the valley of Lebanon" (Josh. 11:17; 12:7).

"Under Hermon" is also the description of the land of Mizpeh (Josh. 11:3 [RSV: Mizpah]), which is commonly identified with the valley of Marj-'ayyun. Thus Baal-gad must be sought at the northern end of the land of Mizpeh.[4] Since the valley of Lebanon lies further north, it is reasonable to assume that Baal-gad was located somewhere between the valleys of Mizpeh and Lebanon, thus relating to both areas. The Litani river is a prominent feature of that region, but is not mentioned by this or any other name in the Bible. The only way the biblical writer could regard Baal-gad as the southern end of the valley of Lebanon was by taking the Litani to be part of that valley. For him, Baal-gad marked the southern end of the valley of Lebanon just as Lebo-hamath marked its northern end. Whatever the exact location of Baal-gad, it is probably on the watershed, and it is clear that the border passed along the southern foot of mount Hermon, then turned northwards and encompassed both the source of the Jordan river and the valley of Marj-'ayyun.

4. For the location of Baal-gad, see P.W. Skehan, "Joab's Census: How Far North (2 Sam. 24:6)?", *CBQ*, vol. 31 (1969), pp. 46-47; Wuest, *Untersuchungen*, pp. 39-40.

David's census (2 Sam. 24:6) is described in these words: "Then they came to Gilead, and to ארץ תחתים חדשי and they came to Dan, and from Dan they went around to Sidon." This verse is obviously corrupt. Despite the fact that many distinguished scholars follow proto-Lucian and reconstruct the text as ארץ החתים קדשה (cf. the RSV translation: "Kadesh in the land of the Hittites"), it seems to me preferable to conjecture the original text to have been תחת הר חרמון (below mount Hermon).[5]

The other toponyms mentioned in the verse are Dan and Ijon.[6] It is clear that the limit of the territory in 2 Sam. 24:5-7 is identical with the northern boundary of the Israelite tribal system and, by inference, the northern border of the tribe of Naphtali.[7]

5. In support of this emendation, see Josh. 11:17, 13:5 (cf. also 11:3). Hermon was first suggested by H. Ewald (*Geschichte des Volkes Israel*, third edition (Goettingen 1866), vol. 3, p. 220 n. 1. English translation by J.E. Carpenter, *The History of Israel*, second edition (London 1878), vol. 3, p. 162 n. 3) and improved upon by H. Graetz, *Emendationes in Plerosque Sacrae Scripturae Veteris Testamenti Libros* (Breslau 1892), p. 28. K. Budde (*Die Buecher Samuel, Kurzer Hand Commentar zum AT*, Abteilung VIII (Tuebingen und Leipzig 1902), p. 329) is unable to accept the emendation, much as he would like to do so; and Driver, *Samuel*, p. 374 says that Hermon "certainly yields a more probable locality". For a more recent attempt to justify this reading, see Skehan, ibid., [note 4 above], p. 45 n. 16.

6. The MT דנה יען does not make sense, neither do the versions. There have been several proposals for emendation. Since the LXX seems to reflect a text where Dan is mentioned more than once, J. Wellhausen (*Der Text der Buecher Samuelis* (Goettingen 1871), p. 218) suggested ויבאו דנה ומדן סבבו (and they came to Dan, and from Dan they circled...). Tempting as this may be, I prefer the emendation of A. Klosterman (*Die Buecher Samuelis und der Koenige, Kurzgefasster Kommentar zu den Heiligen Schriften des Alten und Neuen Testaments* (Noerdlingen 1887), p. 256; cf. also K. Budde, op. cit. [note 5 above], p. 330) who proposed a metathesis of יען - עין (plena עיון) reading ויבאו דנה ועיון ויסבו...... This refers, no doubt, to Ijon which is north of Dan (1 Kings 15:20; cf. also 2 Kings 15:29).

7. W. Fuss ("II Samuel 24", ZAW, vol. 74 (1962), pp. 145-164, esp., p. 151) has put forward that 2 Sam. 24:5-7 is an early interpolation. This was taken one step further by Wuest (*Untersuchungen,* pp. 142-143, 166) and H. Donner ("The interdependence of Internal Affairs and Foreign Policy during the Davidic-Solomonic Period, with special Regard to the Phoenician Coast", in: Ishida, *Studies,* pp. 209-212) who postulated literary dependency of 2 Sam 24:5-7 on Josh. 13 and 19. However, it is preferable to assume that the boundary descriptions (Josh. 13:16, 25; 19:29, 37) and Joab's journey (2 Sam. 24:5-7) were independent of one another, and that the similarities between them are the result of a similar geographical setting and historical background, rather than literary influence. Even though it is an interpolation, the passage must have belonged to an early document used by the redactor, and can therefore serve as a reliable source for the study of the extent of David's Kingdom.

The question that arises is, why was Naphtali's northern border, as well as several important cities in that same area (Ijon, Dan and Abel-beth-maacah), omitted from the description in Josh. 19:32-34? I believe that the explanation lies in the overall historical concept of the writer who drew up the entire boundary system. According to him, the whole land was divided among the twelve tribes. The inheritance of Dan, situated in the centre of the country, was part of this system. But the writer was also aware of a second half of the tribe of Dan living north of Naphtali, between Abel-beth-maacah and Ijon (Josh. 19:47).[8] His basic scheme precluded counting a second tribe of Dan in the north, since the two halves of Manasseh were regarded as one tribe. Nor could he assign a city named Dan to the territory of Naphtali. In order to avoid these difficulties he ignored the northern territory of Dan altogether (Josh. 19:34; cf. LXX "...and reached Asher on the west and the Jordan on the east"). Thus a gap remained between Naphtali's land and the northern boundary of the tribal inheritances. This can be reconstructed from other descriptions of the northern border.[9]

8. The author of 1 Kings 15:20 distinguished between the three cities of Ijon, Dan and Abel-beth-maacah and the rest of the territory of Naphtali. One may suggest that the territory occupied by the Danites enclosed this trio, which exactly matches the missing portion of the inheritance of Naphtali in the north.

9. Noth ("Studien", pp. 227-228; *Josua,* pp. 14, 77, 120-123) has suggested that the northern half of Dan was included in the original document of the boundary system and that a later redactor, who

Modern historical geography followed Alt in excluding the inheritance of Dan from the boundary system.[10] However, strong arguments were suggested by Cross and Wright,[11] for its inclusion, and the present author has found further arguments supporting their views.[12] These will be discussed in the next chapter. Suffice it to state here that the basic concept of the boundary system dividing the land among twelve tribes, as well as the territorial gap between the border descriptions of Dan's neighbours (Judah, Benjamin and Ephraim) and the external southwestern limits of the country, lead to the conclusion that Dan was an integral part of the system. The suggestion that the omission of the Danite territory in the north can be explained only by assuming that Dan was part of the tribal allotments may strengthen this claim.[13]

annexed the southern half of Dan to the boundary system, left it out. However, Josh. 19:33, which according to Noth delineated Naphtali's northern border, clearly describes its southern border (Kallai, *Tribes,* pp. 193-195). Thus, the missing northern boundary of Naphtali - regardless of whether it was located south of the tribe of Dan or north of it - is not explained by Noth's theory.

10. Kallai, *Tribes,* pp. 304-312, with further literature; Strange, "Dan".

11. Cross-Wright, "Boundary", pp. 202-211.

12. Na'aman, "Amarna", pp. 80-85.

13. Those who omitted the southern half of Dan from the boundary system were unable to explain the absence from it of both the northern half of Dan and the northern boundary of Naphtali. See Aharoni, *LB,* p. 239; Kallai, *Tribes,* pp. 260, 367, 370 [cf. note 9 above].

b) The Location of Misrephoth-maim

Misrephoth-maim is mentioned only twice in the Bible: in the descriptions of "the land that yet remains" (Josh. 13:6) and of the pursuit following the battle at the waters of Merom (Josh. 11:8). Several scholars have identified Misrephoth-maim with Khirbet Musheirefeh, at the northern end of the plain of Acco.[14] However, this site does not fit the geographical context of either of the verses. Aharoni has suggested identifying it with the estuary of the Litani river south of the kingdom of Sidon.[15] Kallai, on the other hand, suggested that Misrephoth-maim be sought at the northern end of the kingdom of Sidon.[16] Before discussing these suggestions one must consider the basic question: in which main direction is "all the inhabitants of the hill country from Lebanon to Misrephoth-maim..." (Josh. 13:6) to be placed? Locating Misrephoth-maim either to the south or to the north of Sidon presupposes an east-west direction of the toponyms. But the very concept of the remaining land was designed to bridge the gap between the Land of Canaan and the

14. Aharoni, *LB*, p. 216 n. 109; id., "Misrephoth-maim", *EM*, vol. 5 (1968), p. 641 [Hebrew].

15. Aharoni, ibid.; F. M. Abel ("Oronte et Litani", *JPOS*, vol. 13 (1933), pp. 156-158) demonstrated that the river was called Litani from the earliest times. Since Aharoni (*LB*, pp. 171, 216 n. 111) adopted this proposition his identification of Misrephoth-maim with the Litani river has little to recommend it.

16. Kallai, "Boundaries", p. 31 n. 24.

tribal boundaries. Toponyms arranged from east to west would have been of no value in delineating this territorial gap. It is therefore more reasonable to assume a north-south arrangement of the toponyms, exactly as in all the other references in this chapter to the remaining land.

It seems to me that Josh. 13:6 refers to the mountain region between the two other pairs of toponyms mentioned in verses 4-5, but in reverse order, i.e., north to south. This would clarify the description in Josh. 11:8. Chapter 11 recounts the conquest of the north of the country, as far as the boundary of the tribal inheritances, parallel to chapter 10, which describes the conquest of the south.[17] The three toponyms mentioned in chapter 11 (Sidon the Great, Misrephoth-maim and the valley of Mizpeh) run from west to east along the northern line of the boundary system. Misrephoth-maim must be located somewhere on the Litani river, on the (missing) northern border of Naphtali's inheritance. There is a place called Serifah approximately two km. south of the river, 17 km. west of Tyre (map reference 187.298), but the site and its surroundings have not yet been investigated. Pending a thorough survey of this area, it is better not to suggest an exact location.

However, locating Misrephoth-maim somewhere along the Litani river fits admirably into the line described in Josh. 11:8. This would pass north of the Marj-'ayyun valley as far

17. De Vaux, *Early History*, pp. 655-656; Roesel, "Kriege", pp. 171-183.

as the Litani river and continue westward along it. Thus, Misrephoth-maim was not, as suggested by many scholars, part of Asher's inheritance, which is why there is no mention of it in the description of the tribe's border.

c) Sidon the Great and the Borders of Tyre and Sidon

According to the description of the inheritance of Asher (Josh. 19:28-29), the border ran from the south northwards "as far as Sidon the Great", turned sharply (*šb*) to Ramah and reached the spring[18] of the fortress of Tyre. Then it turned sharply again, passed through Hosah, and reached the sea.[19] Sidon the Great marks the northwestern end of the pursuit recounted in Josh. 11:8. In 2 Sam. 24:6-7 we are told that David's censors "...came to Dan, and from Dan they went around to Sidon, and came to the fortress of Tyre...". Here Sidon is identical with Sidon the Great.[20]

18. Read with LXX *'yn* instead of MT *'yr*. See Steuernagel, *Josua*, p. 228; Cooke, *Joshua*, pp. 180-181.

19. Noth's suggestion (*Josua*, pp. 114, 119), accepted by Schmitt (*Frieden*, p. 62), that part of Josh. 19:28-29 was interpolated is not well founded. Nor is their demarcation of the northern boundary of the Israelite kingdom in the time of the United Monarchy acceptable.

20. The phrase צידון רבה appears only twice in the MT – Josh. 11:8 and 19:28 (LXX[A.L.] has it also in 2 Sam 24:6). The use of *rbh* (the great) seems to indicate that the kingdom, not the city, of Sidon is meant. But quite often 'Sidon' without any qualification serves the same purpose - e.g., Judg. 18:28; 1 Kings

It has often been suggested that the Litani river marks the northern border of Asher and that Sidon was outside its inheritance.[21] Kallai, however, believes that Sidon was included within the tribal territory.[22] The two views are based on different verses.

17:9. I cannot explain why in Josh. 19:28 the RSV translates "Sidon the Great" (as it does in Amos 6:2 for חמת רבה = "Hamath the great") whereas in Josh. 11:8 the same phrase is translated as "Great Sidon".
The term *rbh* is quite common in the Syro-Palestinian onomasticon, especially in pairs of 'great and...'. In the annals of Sennacherib there appear "Great Sidon" and "Little Sidon", and scholars have suggested that these refer either to two different places or to two quarters of the city of Sidon. In the topographical list of Thutmes III we find "Great 'pr" and "Little 'pr" (nos. 53-54). The topographical list of Shishak contains "Great Arad" (nos. 108-109) and "Arad nbt" (nos. 110-111). Three pairs of "great" and "rich in water" are mentioned in the Ugaritic texts, two of them in the Keret Epic (see M. Astour, "A North Mesopotamian Locale of the Keret Epic?", *Ugarit Forschungen*, vol. 5 (1973), p. 32).
Sidon and Sidonians are used in the Bible as names for both the land and its inhabitants. The names 'Sidon' and 'Sidon the Great' can be used interchangeably in the descriptions of the northern border of the tribes of Israel, and in this context both names designate the entire territory of the kingdom of Sidon.

21. Aharoni, *LB*, p. 238; Kallai, *Tribes*, pp. 180-181, with further literature in nn. 236, 237.

22. Kallai, *Tribes*, p. 181; id., "Boundaries", pp. 29-31; cf. Schmitt, *Frieden*, p. 62.

The text describing the remaining land along the northern coast (Josh. 13:4-5) seems to be corrupt. The first word *mtmn* (in the south) undoubtedly belongs to the end of the previous verse. One would then expect "all the land of the Canaanites" to be defined as usual by means of the construction "from... to...". Several commentators have therefore assumed a haplography, and proposed that *m'rh* be read *mm'rh.*[23] Indeed, in Judg. 3:3 (cf. LXX of Josh. 13:4), the Sidonians appear among the foreign elements within the remaining land. The next expression in Josh. 13:4, "to Aphek", is generally identified with the town of Afqa in the Lebanon, situated at the source of Nahr Ibrahim.[24] Malamat suggests identifying Mearah

23. Buhl, op. cit., [note 2 above], p. 54; Steuernagel, *Josua,* p. 200; Cooke, *Joshua,* p. 119. But even without haplography, merely by altering the punctuation, one can read וּמֵעָרָה (and from 'Ara). See D. Barthelemy, *Critique Textuelle de l'Ancien Testament,* Part I, Orbis Biblicus et Orientalis, vol. 50/51 (Fribourg/Goettingen 1982), pp. 27-28. The location of such an assumed 'Ara is unknown. Abel's suggestion ("La Prétendue Caverne des Sidoniens et la Localisation de la Ville de 'Ara", *RB,* vol. 58 (1951), pp. 47-53) to locate this 'Ara in the 'Aruna pass, south of Megiddo, is out of the question. Cf. Baldi, op. cit., [note 2 above], pp. 96-99.

24. The suggested identification of this Aphek by R. North ("Ap(h)eq(a) and 'Azeqa", *Biblica,* vol. 41 (1960), p. 52) and M. Dothan ("Aphek on the Israel-Aram Border and Aphek on the Amorite Border", *Eretz Israel,* vol. 12 (1975), pp. 63-65 [Hebrew]), is in my opinion untenable.

(the cave) with the famous grotto of Adonis near Afqa.[25] Since the construction "from...to...to..." shows that Mearah and Aphek were at opposite ends of the territory in question, they could not possibly have been neighbours. The site of Mearah must therefore have been south of the kingdom of Sidon, near the Litani river or even further south.[26]

The second half of the verse (Josh. 13:4) is also corrupt. Its original text would appear to have included all the area from south of the kingdom of Sidon (or even south of Tyre) as far north as the border of the land of the Amorites. This area included two territories, mentioned from south to north: the kingdoms of Sidon and of Byblos. Afqa was on the southern edge of the kingdom of Byblos, whose northern edge was the border with the land of the Amorites.[27] Thus the southern

25. A. Malamat, "Recension: *Histoire ancienne d'Israel: Des origines a l'installation en Canaan*, par R. de Vaux", *RB*, vol. 80 (1973), pp. 84-85.

26. For the various locations proposed for the 'cave' of the Sidonians, see Cooke, *Joshua*, pp. 119-120; Abel, *Geographie* p. 381.

27. This name is a survival from the kingdom of Amurru of the Late Bronze Age. See de Vaux, *Early History*, p. 131; M. Liverani, "The Amorites", in: *Peoples of Old Testament Times*, ed. D.J. Wiseman (Oxford 1973), pp. 123-124. Otherwise, see Aharoni (*LB*, pp. 64, 67, 213, 217), who marked Aphek as the northern border of the Land of Canaan, although the boundary of Amurru was much further north.

border of the land of the Amorites (which is Nahr el-Kebir = the Eleutheros river of classical sources) was the north-western border of the Land of Canaan.[28]

One is now tempted to reconstruct the original text of Josh 13:4-5 as follows: All the land of the Canaanites from Mearah which belongs to the Sidonians to Aphek, and the land of the Gebalites to the boundary of the Amorites. Whether or not that is correct, the kingdom of Sidon certainly lay within the remaining land.

Other descriptions of the northern border provide further support for the assumption that Sidon was outside the boundary system. By combining the tradition of Josh. 11:8 and 2 Sam. 24:6, it becomes clear that the border of the tribes ran westwards along the Litani river. The words "around to Sidon" (2 Sam. 24:6) were intended to describe a detour around Sidon from the south, subsequently reaching the fortress of Tyre, which marked the extreme north-western boundary of the kingdom. The same is true of the boundary of Asher. This reached the Litani river, which formed the southern border of Sidon and turned west along it to the spring at the foot of the fortress of Tyre, at the north-eastern corner of that kingdom. At this point the border of Asher turned south along the eastern boundary of the kingdom of Tyre, to the coast south of it,

28. For the southern border of Amurru, see G. Kestemont, "Le Nahr el-Kebir et le pays d'Amurru", *Berytus*, vol. 20 (1971), pp. 47-55.

through a place called Hosah.[29] The territory of Tyre west of the border of Asher roughly corresponds with the city-state of Tyre, as known from Late Bronze Age documents, in particular the Amarna Letters.[30] It is clear, therefore, that the kingdoms of both Tyre and Sidon remained outside the allotments of the Israelite tribes (i.e., David's kingdom at its peak).

One may conclude that both the northern and north-western borders of Asher were amply described, because they were the external boundaries of the kingdom at that time. The same is true of the south-western border with the kingdoms of Philistia (Josh. 15:10b-11).

The cities of Asher appear in the list of the unconquered Canaanite cities (Judg. 1:21, 27-35). This passage is, in my opinion, a register of the important Canaanite towns captured by David within the territory of the tribal allotments. The list was intentionally formulated in a negative manner, describing David's conquests as towns which the Israelites had not been

29. For the phonetic difficulties in the identification of Hosah with the town of Usu (the coastal town opposite Tyre, today Tell Rashidiyeh), see S.E. Loewenstamm, "Hosah", *EM,* vol. 3 (1958), pp. 223-224 [Hebrew]; Kallai, *Tribes,* pp. 183-184. The same phonetic difficulties appear in the identification of "Hobah north of Damascus" (Gen. 14:15) with the Upi in documents of the second millennium B.C., (see B. Mazar, "Hobah", *EM,* vol. 3 (1958), p. 44 [Hebrew]).

30. H.J. Katzenstein, *The History of Tyre* (Jerusalem 1973), p. 29.

able to conquer in the past. The order and the description of these cities, arranged according to tribal territories, fully accords with the boundary system both in time and in delineation [see chapter 2 pp. 95-98].[31]

The inclusion of Sidon among the unconquered cities of Asher (Judg. 1:31) was taken by Kallai as proof that the border of Asher lay north of the kingdom of Sidon.[32] However, our delineation of the northern tribal boundary contradicts this assumption. If Kallai were correct, where are the important Sidonian cities (such as Zarephath) in the list of the unconquered Canaanite cities? Furthermore, the borders of David's kingdom as reflected in 2 Sam. 24 exclude all the neighbouring kingdoms (Philistia, Moab, Ammon, Aram, and Tyre). The same picture prevailed in the Solomonic district system (1 Kings 4:7-19) and in the enumeration of Solomon's foreign women (1 Kings 11:1). Although some of the verses about David's conquests regarding the treatment of several captured kingdoms are ambiguous (2 Sam. 8:6, 14; 12:30-31), it is evident that he did not annex any of the well-established neighbouring kingdoms. Why, then, should he treat the old

31. For the list of unconquered Canaanite cities, see Kallai, *Tribes*, pp. 90-96, with further literature on p. 90 n. 9; Aharoni, *LB*, pp. 212-215; Schmitt, *Frieden*, pp. 53-80; A.G. Auld ("Judges 1 and History: A Reconsideration", *VT*, vol. 25 (1975), pp. 279-284) suggested that the list of unconquered Canaanite cities is mainly dependent on the parallel in the book of Joshua.

32. Kallai, *Tribes*, p. 181.

kingdom of Sidon differently? After all, Sidon and the Sidonians are regarded everywhere in the Bible as a nation alien to Israel. All these arguments preclude the possibility that Sidon was ever included within the tribal allotments.

The case for the inclusion of the Sidonians among the unconquered cities of Asher should be discussed in the light of this conclusion. For the sake of clarity, we shall juxtapose the places mentioned in the list of unconquered Canaanite cities and in Asher's town list.[33]

Judg. 1:31		Josh. 19:29-30
the inhabitants of	Acco	-----
the inhabitants of	Sidon	-----
or of	Ahlab	*(m)hbl*
or of	Achzib	Achzib
or of	Helbah	[Acco][34]
or of	Aphik	Aphek
or of	Rehob	Rehob

33. Aharoni (*LB*, p. 214) suggested that the "inhabitants of Sidon" in the list of unconquered Canaanite cities (Judg. 1:31) is a general designation for the inhabitants of the plain of Acco, who at the time of the United Monarchy were regarded as Sidonians. But the plain of Acco was considered in this list as part of the inheritance of Asher, while Sidon and Tyre as part of the remaining land. Only after the plain of Acco was transferred to Tyre during the second half of Solomon's reign could its inhabitants be regarded as Sidonians.

The similar sequence of the two lists is not accidental, but there is also a marked difference between them. In place of Acco, located in its proper geographical position in Josh. 19, in Judg. 1:31 the unknown toponym Helbah (which is probably a variation of Ahlab) appears while Acco heads the list and is followed by Sidon.[35] This anomaly may have been the work of an interpolator, who transferred Acco from its proper place and inserted Sidon, both with the addition "the inhabitants of" (the LXX also added here "the inhabitants of Dor and the inhabitants of..."). One might suggest that this interpolator was trying to 'up-date' the list of the unconquered cities of the northern coast by starting with the most important cities of his time, Sidon, Acco and Dor. To these he attached the words "the inhabitants of" to emphasize their importance. Although this is no more than a theory, it could explain how Sidon (and possibly Dor) was included in a list to which it did not originally belong.[36]

34. So some MSS of LXX, see A.E. Brooke and N. McLean, *The Old Testament in Greek*, vol. 1 (Cambridge 1917), ad loc. MT has עמה, which indicates, as J. Hollenberg ("Zur Textkritik des Buches Josua und des Buches der Richter", *ZAW*, vol. 1 (1881), pp. 100-101) pointed out that Acco was here spelt עכה, whereas usually it is written עכו. Cf. also A. Dillmann, *Die Buecher Numeri, Deuteronomium und Josua, Kurzgefasstes exegetisches Handbuch zum AT*, second edition (Leipzig 1886), p. 562.

35. G.F. Moore, *A Critical and Exegetical Commentary on Judges*, *ICC* (Edinburgh 1895), pp. 49-50; C.F. Burney, *The Book of Judges with Introduction and Notes* (London 1918; reprinted New York 1970), p. 28.

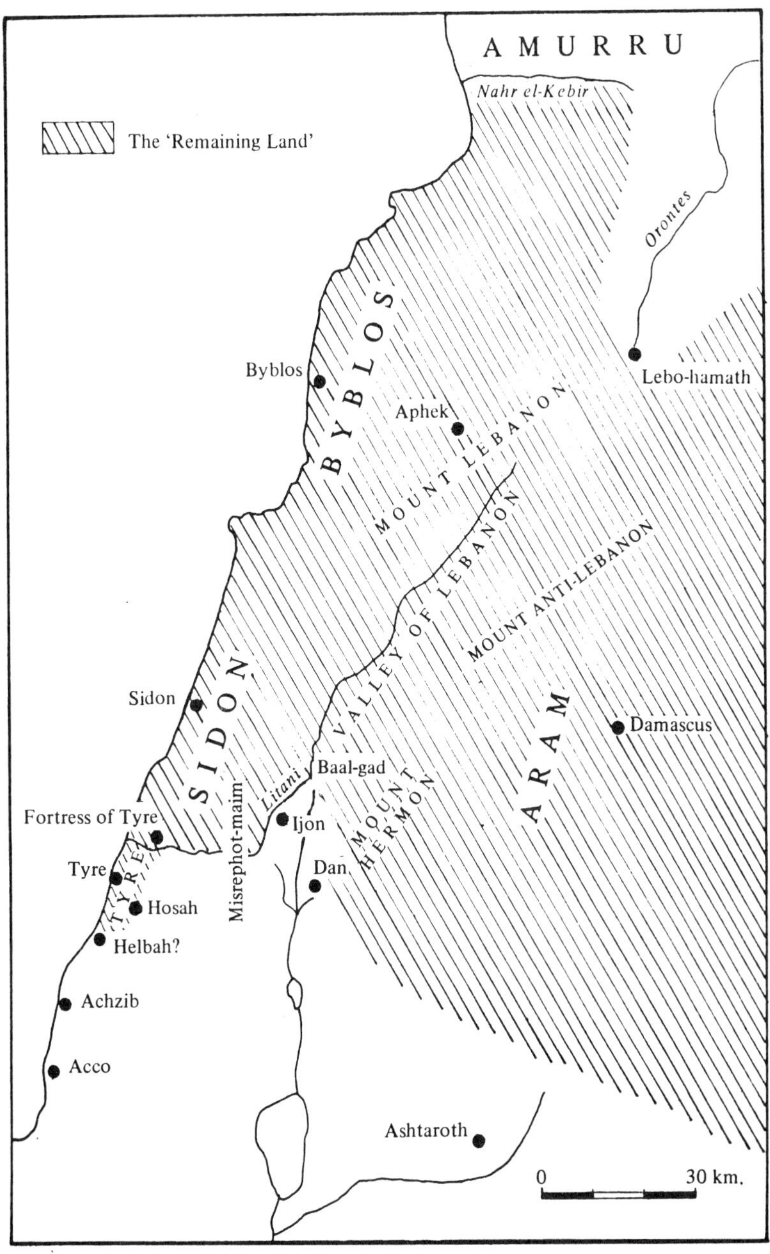

Map 1. The Remaining Land.

The city of *hbl* (Helbah? Ahlab?), which heads the original list of towns, should in my opinion be located south of the borders of the kingdom of Tyre. It has nothing to do with the city of Mahalliba (Khirbet el-Mahalib), mentioned in the annals of Sennacherib, which was situated near the mouth of the Litani river within the kingdom of Tyre.[37] It can tentatively be located at Ras el-Abyad (the *Promontorium Album* of Pliny), 12 km. south of Tyre near the border of that kingdom.[38] The end of Josh. 19:29 may be translated thus: from Helbah/Ahlab to Achzib.

This delineation of the northern border of the boundary system strongly supports the proposition that the inheritances of the twelve tribes reflect the boundaries of the Israelite kingdom at the time of the United Monarchy. In no other period was the northern coastal region an integral part of the Israelite realm [see chapter 5 pp. 178-179].

The possible time-span for the composition of the tribal allotments might even be narrowed. According to 1 Kings 9:10-13, Solomon gave Hiram of Tyre twenty towns in the

36. Schmitt, *Frieden*, pp. 60, 62-63.

37. This is contrary to the commonly held opinion. See e.g., Cooke, *Joshua*, p. 181; Noth, *Josua*, pp. 114-119; Aharoni, *LB*, p. 214; cf. Kallai, *Tribes*, pp. 186-188.

38. This was already suggested by Moore, op. cit., [note 35 above], pp. 49-51.

land of Cabul. Parts of the Acco plain may previously have been annexed by the king of Tyre; Solomon's yielding the land of Cabul being the final step in the chain of events. The original loss of these territories may be connected with the campaign of Pharaoh Siamun against Israel in the early days of Solomon, perhaps immediately after the death of David (1 Kings 9:16). The main purpose of that campaign was to re-establish Egyptian power and influence in the former Land of Canaan, and particularly on the coast of Philistia and in Phoenicia, two traditional centres of interest for Egypt. The campaign was a success from the Egyptian point of view, since the resulting peace treaty reinforced by a marriage alliance (1 Kings 3:1; 7:8; 9:16, 24; 11:1; 2 Chr. 8:11), was accompanied by Solomon's withdrawal from parts of the northern and southern coasts of his kingdom. Egypt retained its hold on the coast of Philistia. In the days of Rehoboam this was to enable Pharaoh Shishak to march unopposed along the southern coast.[39] The rest of the northern coast, i.e., the land of Cabul, was transferred to the kingdom of Tyre by Solomon, probably as a part of an economic pact (1 Kings 5:8-10 [=MT 5:22-24]).

39. For the various explanations of the Egyptian campaign and of Solomon's marriage to the daughter of Pharaoh, see the extensive literature referred to in N. Na'aman, "Hebron Was Built Seven Years Before Zoan in Egypt (Numbers XIII 22)", *VT*, vol. 31 (1981), p. 492 nn. 10 and 12; also A.R. Schulman, "Diplomatic Marriage in the Egyptian New Kingdom", *JNES*, vol. 38 (1979), pp. 177-193; A. Malamat, "A Political Look at the Kingdom of David and Solomon and Its Relations with Egypt", in: Ishida, *Studies*, pp. 198-204.

The cession of the land of Cabul was one more step in the dissolution of David's empire. This is the background for the rebuilding of Hazor, Megiddo and Gezer (1 Kings 9:15). The three cities were fortified as a result of withdrawal on three main fronts: the Damascene (1 Kings 11:24-25), the Tyrian and that of Philistia. Thus, the boundary system reflects the maximum borders of the United Monarchy at the end of David's and the beginning of Solomon's reigns.

3) The Inheritance of Judah and the Southern Border of the Remaining Land

On the assumption that the kingdom of Sidon was included within the confines of both the remaining land and the inheritance of Asher, Kallai propounded a division of the former territory into (a) the alloted parts of the remaining land (i.e., areas which were included both in the inheritances of the tribes and in the remaining land); and (b) the unassigned parts of that land.[40] Sidon in the north and the coast of Philistia in the south come into the first category.

We have already shown that all the remaining land in the north was outside the tribal inheritances. In the south, however, the coast of Philistia was included both within the remaining land (Josh. 13:2-3) and within the inheritance of Judah (Josh. 15:2-4). This anomalous situation demands attention. Since the problems relating to the southern border of Canaan have already been discussed in great detail by the

40. Kallai, "Boundaries", p. 32.

present writer,[41] only the geographical relationship of the remaining land and the inheritance of Judah will be considered here.

The divergence between the borders of the Land of Canaan and the inheritances of the Israelite tribes, in both the north and the east, is very clear. The borders of the Land of Canaan reached Lebo-hamath (Num. 34:7-8; Josh. 13:4-5) and Nahr el-Kebir in the north [see above pp. 53-54], while the borders of the tribes only reached mount Hermon and the Litani river. The borders of the Land of Canaan reached the Jordan in the east (Num. 34:12), while those of the tribes included parts of Transjordan, extending as far as the neighbouring kingdoms of Moab, Ammon and Aram.

In the south, however, the two sets of borders are identical. This is indeed surprising, since it does not fit the rationale either of the Land of Canaan or of the tribal inheritances. The borders of the former reflect the limits of permanent settlement in the Late Bronze Age and were rooted in a territorial concept which had already started in the Middle Bronze Age.[42] The inclusion within these boundaries of the

41. Na'aman, "Brook"; id., "Shihor".

42. Mazar, "Lebo", p. 93; Aharoni, *LB*, pp. 68-69; R. de Vaux, "Le Pays de Canaan", in: *Essays in Memory of E.A. Speiser*, ed. W.W. Hallo, American Oriental Series, vol. 53 (New Haven 1968), [= *JAOS*, vol. 88 (1968)], pp. 28-29; Na'aman, "Brook", pp. 76-77; id., "Shihor", p. 97.

desert areas south of the Beer-sheba valley, which were uninhabited throughout the second millennium B.C., therefore seems very strange.

The tribal inheritances reflect the borders of David's kingdom at its zenith, leaving the vassal states outside their confines. The inclusion of the coast of Philistia within the territory of the tribe of Judah is remarkable: It was never annexed to the kingdom of Israel (cf. 1 Kings 2:39-40), and it was not included either in the description of David's census (2 Sam. 24), or in the Solomonic districts (1 Kings 4).

One may suggest that it was under the influence of the boundary system that the triangular desert area, with Kadesh-barnea at its southern extremity, was artificially annexed to the Land of Canaan; and that it was under the influence of the concept of the Land of Canaan that the coast of Philistia was similarly attached to the inheritance of Judah.

The responsibility for this consistency in the border descriptions rests, in my opinion, with the Judaean writer, who's aim was to extend the territory of his tribe - which was also the king's tribe - as far as possible and to legitimize the Judaean hold on these recently-acquired territories. There are several other cases in which the hands of Judaean writers trying to adapt historical reality in favour of their own tribe can be detected. Only a few examples need be given here. An early conquest of the coast of Philistia (Judg. 1:18) and the city of Jerusalem (Judg. 1:8) was ascribed to the tribe of Judah, although it is well known that both areas were captured by David. The subjugation of the southern desert area between Kadesh-barnea and Gaza was ascribed to Joshua (Josh. 10:41), though this territory was first subordinated during the time of the United Monarchy. The tribe of Judah was excluded from the list of tribes and their unconquered Canaanite cities (Judg. 1:21, 27-35) in order to emphasize its success in driving out the Canaanites. The tribe of Simeon has an independent place in the scheme of the twelve tribal inheritances;[43] nevertheless, in the boundary system its inheritance was included within the confines of the tribe of Judah. In the same manner, in the cycle of stories about David's days, the name 'Negeb of Judah' was attached to the area inhabited by the sons of Simeon. All these distortions have a common purpose: to legitimize Judah's hold on the inheritance ascribed to it in the boundary system by emphasizing that the whole of it had been in its possession ever since the occupation of the land.

Several other cases demonstrate the bias of the Judaean writers. A remarkable one is the description of Absalom's rebellion, in which the tribe of Judah took the major part. The Judaean writer was reluctant to blame his own tribe for the rebellion. He therefore consistently used the terms 'the men of Israel' and 'all the men of Israel' for the followers of Absalom, until he came to the point where the tribe of Judah again supported their king. Thereafter he called them 'the men of

43. Na'aman, "Simeon", pp. 143-147.

Judah' and 'Judah'.[44] The tribe of Judah was interpolated into Judg. 20:18 in order to stress the primacy of Judah amongst the Israelite tribes.[45] On the other hand, Judah was omitted from the district system (1 Kings 4:7-19) in order to conceal the fact that the tribe was included within the heavy taxation imposed by Solomon on his subjects [see chapter 5 p. 176].

This bias of the Judaean writers may explain the curious inclusion, contrary to historical fact, of the coast of Philistia within the boundary of the tribe of Judah.

One may conclude that the remaining land encompassed only those territories which remained outside the tribal allotments. Its border north of Philistia (Josh. 13:2-3) was identical to the line from Beth-shemesh to the Mediterranean of Josh. 15:10b-11, describing the western portion of Judah's northern boundary.

44. For the part played by the tribe of Judah in Absalom's rebellion, see H. Bardtke, "Erwaegungen zur Rolle Judas im Aufstand des Absalom", in: *Wort und Geschichte, Festschrift fuer K. Elliger,* AOAT, vol. 18 (1973), pp. 1-8; Cruesemann, *Widerstand,* pp. 94-104, with earlier literature.

45. With regard to the primacy of the tribe of Judah in the book of Judges, see A.G. Auld, "Review of Boling's *Judges:* The Framework of Judges and the Deuteronomists", *JSOT,* no. 1 (1976), p. 45.

This conclusion is supported by the conflicting concepts of Kadesh-barnea in biblical traditions. On the one hand, according to Num. 34:4 and Ezek. 47:19, Kadesh-barnea was part of the Land of Canaan conquered by Joshua (Josh. 10:41). On the other hand, the long sojourn at Kadesh-barnea was regarded as a respite outside the borders of Canaan (Ex. 16:35; Josh. 5:12) while spies were sent north to explore it (Num. 13:1-2, 17, 25-26). Furthermore, in numerous biblical traditions the Negeb of Judah was regarded as the southernmost region of Canaan (see e.g., Gen. 10:19; 13:1; Num. 13:17, 22, 29; 21:1; Judg. 1:9), whereas Kadesh-barnea was considered to be in the desert area (Gen. 16:7; 21:14; Num. 13:26; 1 Kings 19:3-4), situated south of the borders of Canaan. All these contradictions result from Judaean writers' artificial inclusion of Kadesh-barnea and the surrounding desert within the Land of Canaan.

The position of Josh. 13:2-6 in its present context should now be considered. This passage has long been regarded as an interpolation.[46] Its background has been discussed in

46. A. Dillmann, *Die Buecher Numeri, Deuteronomium und Josua, Kurzgefasstes Exegetisches Handbuch zum AT* (Leipzig 1886), p. 507; H. Holzinger, *Das Buch Josua, Kurzer Hand-Commentar zum AT* (Tuebingen und Leipzig 1901), p. 49; Noth, *Josua*, pp. 73-74.

great detail by Smend.[47] He suggests that it was interpolated in the course of a second Deuteronomistic revision (called by him DtrN) of the original Deuteronomistic historical work (DtrG) and that several other passages in the books of Joshua and Judges – Josh. 1:7-9; 23:1-16; Judg. 1:2 - 2:5; 2:17, 20-21, 23; 3:1-6 – should also be assigned to this second revision. In Smend's view the passage under discussion may have belonged to an early document used by the redactor for his work, though this is by no means certain.[48]

When examining Josh. 13:2-6 and Judg. 1 it is important to bear in mind how different these descriptions are from the territorial concepts of the Deuteronomist, and how irrelevant to his historical picture.

(a) The territory of the historical Land of Canaan extended to the Jordan, excluding the Transjordanian areas south of the Yarmuk river. This is reflected in Josh. 13:2-6 and Judg. 1. But, according to Deuteronomy, Transjordan is an integral part of the promised land; its conquest beginning with the crossing of

47. R. Smend, "Das Gesetz und die Voelker. Ein Beitrag zur deuteronomistischen Redaktionsgeschichte", in: *Probleme biblischer Theologie, Gerhard von Rad zum 70 Geburtstag,* ed. H.W. Wolff (Muenchen 1971), pp. 494-509 (esp., pp. 497-500); id., "Das uneroberte Land", in: Strecker, *Das Land,* pp. 91-102.

48. Ibid., [note 47 above], pp. 508-509; pp. 100-101 respectively.

the Arnon river (Deut. 2:24, 31-36). Its inhabitants were therefore treated just like the Canaanites, and utterly destroyed (Deut. 2:34-35; 3:6-7).[49]

(b) The borders of the Land of Canaan extended from Lebo-hamath to the Brook of Egypt. But the Deuteronomistic concept of the 'ideal land' which was promised for days to come, extended from the Euphrates to the eastern Nile delta or the gulf of Elath (Gen. 15:18; Ex. 23:31; Deut. 1:7; 11:24; Josh. 1:3-4). This extensive territory was united and organized for the first time under the Assyrians, who introduced the name *eber nari* (Beyond the River). This name reflects the point of view of the people residing east of the Euphrates.

The Deuteronomists used the term *eber nari* for Solomon's empire, thus expanding it far beyond its historical confines (1 Kings 4:21, 24 [= MT 5:1, 4]).[50] David's northernmost conquests encircled the kingdom of Aram-zobah, and reached the southern border of the kingdom of Hamath,

49. M. Weinfeld, "The extent of the Promised Land - the Status of Transjordan", in: Strecker, *Das Land,* pp. 67-68.

50. Na'aman, "Shihor", p. 98; M. Anbar, "Genesis 15: A Conflation of Two Deuteronomic Narratives", *JBL,* vol. 101 (1982), pp. 51-55; T. Veijola, "Davidverheissung und Staatsvertrag", *ZAW,* vol. 95 (1983), pp. 22-29.

near Lebo-hamath. He never actually reached the Euphrates.[51] The Deuteronomistic writers equated the borders of the ideal promised land with those of the United Monarchy, and defined them according to the conditions prevailing in their own time - i.e., *eber nari.*[52]

We may conclude that the detailed descriptions of the remaining land, delineating the territorial gaps between the boundaries of the twelve tribes and the borders of the Land of Canaan, were alien to the imagery of the Deuteronomistic school. The same is true of the account of Judg. 1, which does not fit in with the other descriptions of writers of this school. The author of the chapter emphasized that only Judah and Simeon were able to drive the Canaanites out of their inheritances; the other tribes west of the Jordan failed to do so. Such a tendentious account could only have been composed at a time when the tribe of Judah was struggling to gain hegemony

51. This is contrary to e.g., A. Malamat, "Aspects of the Foreign Policies of David and Solomon", *JNES,* vol. 22 (1963), pp. 1-17; Aharoni, *LB,* pp. 262-264; Weinfeld, ibid., [note 49 above], p. 66.

52. The influence of the boastful style of the Assyrian royal scribes on the biblical geographic formulae of the 7th century B.C., is self evident. See M. Saebo, "Vom Grossreich zum Weltreich", *VT,* vol. 28 (1978), pp. 83-91; Ch. Cohen, "Neo-Assyrian Elements in the First Speech of the Biblical Rab-Shaqe", *Israel Oriental Studies,* vol. 9 (1979), pp. 32-47; P. Machinist, "Assyria and Its Image in the First Isaiah", *JAOS,* vol. 103 (1983), pp. 719-737.

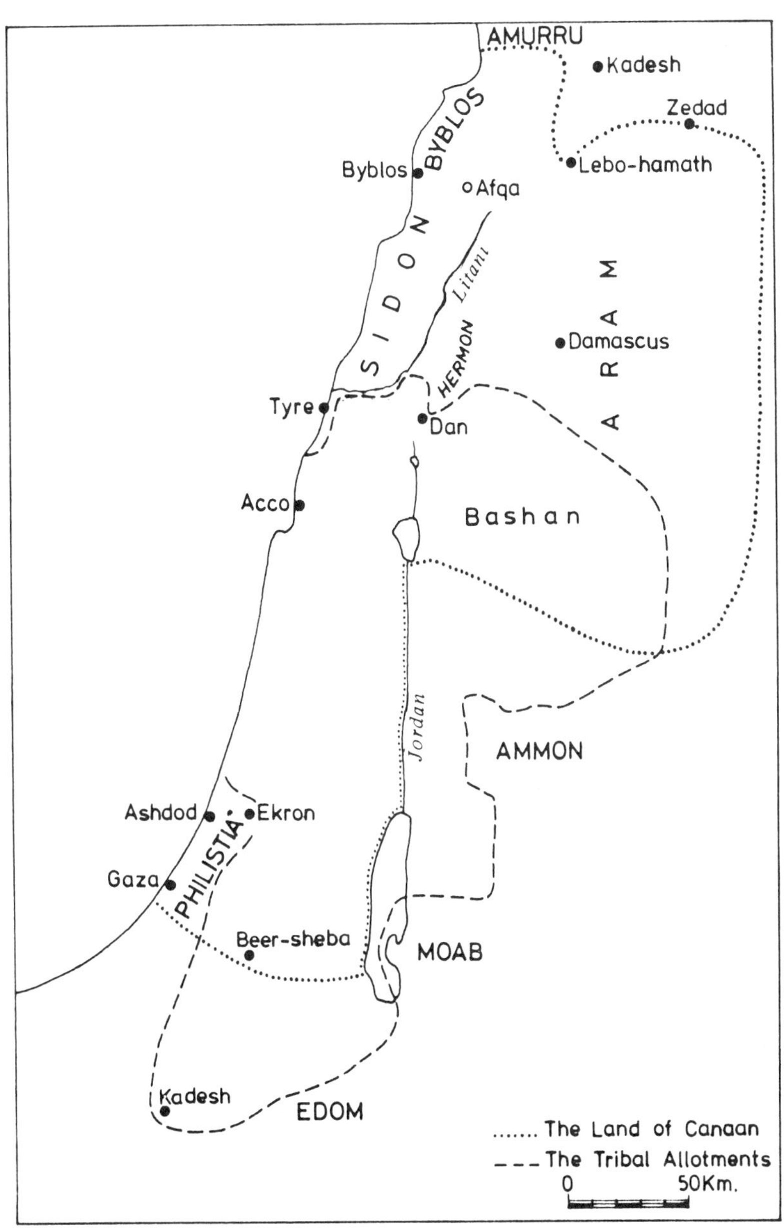

Map 2. The Land of Canaan and the Tribal Allotments.

over the Israelite tribal society. By the time of the second Deuteronomistic revision (DtrN), however, Simeon had already disappeared from the scene, while Judah and Benjamin had been united for hundreds of years. The detailed list of unconquered Canaanite cities within the tribal allotments was no longer significant and there is no logical explanation for the omission of Issachar from a list composed at that time. The emphasis on Judah's (and Simeon's) priority vis à vis the other tribes west of the Jordan certainly fits the early Israelite monarchy.

It is therefore reasonable to assume that the second Deuteronomistic revision used old documents from the time of the Monarchy or perhaps a comprehensive composition of the early history of Israel. Consequently part of the material interpolated by this late revision might be of early date.

To sum up, it can be asserted that numerous biblical passages relating to the tribal inheritances present a uniform concept of borders reflecting an actual situation: the maximum boundaries of the Israelite kingdom during the later years of David's reign. These borders are repeated in the descriptions of Joshua's campaigns (Josh. 10-11), the remaining land, the tribal allotments and David's census, as well as in the list of unconquered Canaanite cities. This conformity enables us to go a step further and suggest that a major composition including all these separate descriptions was written during the United Monarchy. The authors were probably aware of the enormous change in the fortunes of their people and the tremendous importance of the events they were witnessing. They wrote the history of their nation, in an account of unknown nature and scope, which we find merged in the books of the Pentateuch and Former Prophets.[53] Because this account primarily reflects the authors' view of their own time, we can reconstruct from it the geographical disposition of the kingdom of Israel at its zenith in the later years of David.

53. For the book of Genesis, see B. Mazar, "The Historical Background of the Book of Genesis", *JNES*, vol. 28 (1969), pp. 73-83.

CHAPTER TWO

THE INHERITANCE OF DAN AND THE BOUNDARY SYSTEM OF THE TWELVE TRIBES

1) The Inheritance of Dan in Modern Historical Geography

Since Alt's penetrating study "Judas Gaue unter Josia", the inheritance of Dan (Josh. 19:40-46) has not been considered part of the boundary system of the Israelite tribes. Alt's arguments for this exclusion were mainly literary, supplemented by considerations of historical geography. He suggested a clear-cut separation in the book of Joshua between town lists and boundary delineations.

The three southern town lists, Judah (Josh. 15:21-62), Benjamin (Josh. 18:21-28) and Dan (Josh. 19:41-46), were assumed by Alt to have come from an older document, the province list of the kingdom of Judah, which he dates to the time of Josiah. According to him many of the towns of Zebulun, Asher and Naphtali, which appear in the Bible side by side with their boundary delineations (Josh. 19:15, 24-30, 35-38), and all the towns of Issachar (Josh. 19:18-22), were copied from a *Vorlage* of a Galilean town list originating in the Assyrian province of Megiddo.[1]

1. Alt, "Galilaeische Ortsliste", pp. 64-66.

Thus, according to Alt, the original boundary description of the tribes west of the Jordan included only seven tribes (Judah, Benjamin, Ephraim, Manasseh, Zebulun, Asher, Naphtali) and was written during the premonarchial period. The tribes of Simeon, Dan and Issachar had no part in this old document. Simeon's inheritance was included in the inheritance of Judah, the town list of Simeon being a valueless extract from the Judaean town list of Josh. 15.[2] The inheritance of Dan was divided, without any detailed description, between the territories of Judah and Ephraim.[3] Issachar's allotment was originally part of the territory of Manasseh. The absence of the three tribes from the original boundary system and from the closely-connected list of the unconquered Canaanite cities (Judg. 1:21, 27-35) was attributed by Alt either to their lack of an independent status or to their dispersal in the premonarchial period, when these documents were written.[4]

The first scholar to find a flaw in this apparently logical argument was Noth.[5] He maintained that both the towns and

2. Alt, "Judas Gaue", p. 113 n. 4 [=*KS*, vol. 2, pp. 285-286 n. 4]; id., "Beitraege zur historischen Geographie und Topographie des Negeb: III. Saruhen, Ziklag, Horma, Gerar", *JPOS*, vol. 15 (1935), pp. 303-305 [=*KS*, vol. 3, pp. 417-419].

3. Alt, "Galilaeische Ortsliste", p. 66.

4. Alt, "System", pp. 17-24 [=*KS*, vol. 1, pp. 197-202].

5. Noth, "Studien", pp. 208, 228-230.

the border descriptions of the Galilean tribes belong to the original boundary delineations and that Issachar does in fact have a place in the original boundary system of the northern tribes. Although Noth demonstrated most of his claims through his *Grenzfixpunkte* system, an important argument in the case of Issachar was of a different nature. Manasseh's north-eastern boundary adjoins Issachar's territory (Josh. 17:11) and not that of Zebulun, as would be the case if Issachar were missing from the boundary descriptions. This point was further elaborated by Kallai, who suggested that Josh. 17:10-11 should be interpreted thus: "...with the sea as its boundary; this territory was contiguous with Asher on the north and with Issachar on the east. On the border of Issachar and Asher, Manasseh possessed Beth-shean and its dependencies".[6] It should also be noted that the northern border of Manasseh is denoted by a list of towns (Josh. 17:11), and in this respect is similar to the other 'mixed' lists of the Galilean tribes (Zebulun, Asher and Naphtali).

Since Issachar's lot has on its northern side one border description (Josh. 19:22), it too may be considered a 'mixed' list. It is also significant that Issachar had an independent place in the Solomonic district system, which is intimately connected with the boundary system of the Israelite tribes. We may conclude that Issachar's inheritance had an independent position within the boundary system. The appearance of these 'mixed' lists within the boundary system, and particularly the

6. Kallai, *Tribes*, pp. 146-150.

inheritance of Issachar, which is mainly a town list, definitely contradicts Alt's differentiation between border descriptions and town lists.

An important contribution to the clarification of the lot of Dan was made by Cross and Wright.[7] After demonstrating that the Danite town list should be separated from those of Judah and Benjamin, they tried to examine its relation to the other lists of Josh. 13-19. Like the lot of Issachar, Dan's inheritance includes, in addition to the town list, a fragment of a border description (Josh. 19:46). By delineating the western borders of Ephraim, Benjamin and Judah, Cross and Wright were able to demonstrate that the gap remaining between these borders exactly matches Dan's inheritance. Moreover, several Danite towns appear in the list of the unconquered Canaanite cities (Judg. 1:34-35), as is the case with all the other tribes belonging to the boundary system. Accordingly, Cross and Wright concluded that the inheritance of Dan is an integral part of the boundary system of the Israelite tribes.

However, these conclusions have been only partially accepted by other scholars. The exclusion of the Danite list from the town lists of Judah and Benjamin was unanimously admitted, but not its inclusion within the tribal allotments. On the contrary, the Danite inheritance was thereafter treated as a separate, independent list.

7. Cross-Wright, "Boundary", pp. 202-211; cf. Na'aman, "Amarna", pp. 80-85.

This new approach was first advanced by Kallai, who maintained that the biblical inheritance of Dan was actually included within that of Ephraim.[8] Kallai assigned Dan's town list to the time of the United Monarchy. Mazar took this a step further by suggesting two stages for the emergence of the district of Dan: the eastern parts were organized under David, while the western parts were only incorporated in the days of Solomon.[9] Aharoni dated the entire Danite town list to the time of David,[10] while Strange concurs with Alt's dating of it to the time of Josiah, but nevertheless considers it independent of the other contemporary town lists.[11]

The only way to clarify the problem of the Danite inheritance is by considering it along with the other lists.

2) The Date of the Boundary System

Alt maintained that the boundary system originated from the way of life of the Israelite tribes in premonarchial times. He accordingly postulated a single ancient document dating from the period of the Judges and compiled by the central tribal

8. Kallai, "Town Lists", pp. 144-148; id., *Tribes,* pp. 305-307.

9. Mazar, "Dan".

10. Aharoni, *LB,* pp. 266-267.

11. Strange, "Dan".

authorities. This included all the independent tribes west of the Jordan which had well-defined inheritances. The tribal allotments comprised both 'nuclear areas' *(Kerngebiete)*, which were genuine tribal territories, and adjacent regions inhabited or dominated by the Canaanites to which the tribes laid claim. The three dispersed, non-autonomous tribes of Simeon, Dan and Issachar had no place in this original document, and were attached to the boundary system later in order to make it conform with the traditional concept of the twelve tribes of Israel.[12]

This theory was developed by Noth, who maintained that the original document was produced by the Israelite tribal league during the premonarchial period and was formulated as a list of border points.[13] A premonarchial date for the original boundary system was accepted by other scholars, though with divergent views on the number of tribes included in it.[14]

12. Alt, "System", pp. 13-24 [=*KS*, vol. 1, pp. 193-202].

13. Noth, "Ueberlieferung", pp. 161-164.

14. G. von Rad, *Theologie des Alten Testaments*, Band 1 (Muenchen 1958), p. 297 [English translation by D.M.G. Stalker, *Old Testament Theology*, vol. 1 (Edinburgh/London 1962), p. 299]; Aharoni, *LB*, pp. 227-239; Saebo, "Landideal", pp. 34-36; de Geus, *Tribes*, pp. 80-81; de Vaux, *Early History*, pp. 727-730; Schmitt, *Frieden*, pp. 81-86.

Albright, on the other hand, thought that the original boundary system should be dated to the time of David.[15] Mowinckel took his theory a step further: "Hinter einem derartigen 'System' mit seinen politischen und religioesen Forderungen und Theorien und 'Ideologie' liegt die erlebte Tatsache des dawidischen Reiches."[16] Segal dated all the geographical lists of Josh. 13-19 to the time of the United Monarchy.[17] This line of enquiry was pursued by Kallai,[18] who was able to demonstrate by a careful delineation of the borders that the boundary system covers the same area as the borders of the Israelite kingdom under David and Solomon. He also maintained that the administrative division of the

15. Albright, "Issachar", pp. 235-236; id., "Review of M. Noth, *Das Buch Josua*", *JBL*, vol. 57 (1938), p. 226; id., *Religion*, pp. 123-124.

16. Mowinckel, *Quellen*, p. 17; see also id., *Tetrateuch*, pp. 27-32, 51-67.

17. M.H. Segal, "On the Composition of the Book of Joshua", in: *B. Dinaburg Jubilee Volume*, eds., Y. Baer et al. (Jerusalem 1950), pp. 12-13 [Hebrew].

18. Kallai, *Tribes, passim;* id., "United Monarchy". Other scholars have also rejected a premonarchial date for the boundary system. See S. Herrmann, "Autonome Entwicklungen in den Koenigreichen Israel und Juda", *SVT*, vol. 17 (1968), pp. 150-153; A.D.H. Mayes, *Israel in the Period of the Judges*, Studies in Biblical Theology, second series, vol. 29 (London 1974), pp. 67-73; Gottwald, *Tribes*, pp. 155-163, 182-184.

country, as outlined in the list of Solomon's district officers (1 Kings 4:7-19), corresponds exactly with the allotments of the tribes, both representing the territorial situation during the United Monarchy.

Re-examining the claims of Alt and his followers, two basic concepts seem to be unacceptable.

A. The assumption that there was a very high degree of unity and centralized – even institutional – authority among the Israelite tribes in the premonarchial period. This theory has been severely shaken by some recent studies.[19] Noth's hypothetical amphictyonic league does not possess the characteristics that would draw up this kind of document. Only the Israelite kingdom, with its administrative and recording apparatus, its need for legitimation and the emergence

19. See for example: H.M. Orlinsky, "The Tribal System of Israel and Related Groups in the Period of the Judges", *Oriens Antiquus*, vol. 1 (1962), pp. 11-20; G. Fohrer, "Altes Testament – 'Amphiktyonie' und 'Bund'?", *ThLZ*, vol. 91 (1966), pp. 801-816, 893-904 [=*Studien zur alttestamentlichen Theologie und Geschichte*, BZAW, vol. 115 (1969), pp. 84-119] ; R. de Vaux, "La these de l'amphictyonie Israelite", *HThR*, vol. 64 (1971), pp. 415-436; de Geus, *Tribes;* O. Baechli, *Amphiktyonie im Alten Testament: Forschungsgeschichtliche Studie zur Hypothese von Martin Noth* (Basel 1977); N. P. Lemche, "The Greek 'Amphictyony' – Could it be a Prototype for the Israelite Society in the Period of the Judges?", *JSOT*, no. 4 (1977), pp. 48-59.

of a new ideology, could have produced a document dividing the entire land among the tribes of Israel. That land, extending from the Litani river to the Brook of Egypt, and from the boundaries of the Transjordanian kingdoms to the Mediterranean, was far larger than premonarchial Israel.

B. In order to explain the fact that the tribal allotments included areas first conquered and settled during the United Monarchy, Alt suggested that the Israelite tribes could have had claims on surrounding areas even in premonarchial times. In his words: "Damit macht sich in dem System ein starkes theoretisches Interesse geltend, ein Streben nach geographischer Abrundung der unvollkommenen geschichtlichen Tatbestaende...".[20] This theory seems strange. What could have been the purpose of such an unrealistic document in the premonarchial period? One can hardly envisage a document dividing a land as yet partially unoccupied among the members of a hypothetical Israelite tribal league. The idea of a comprehensive document in the premonarchial period is inconceivable. The limits of the tribal allotments correspond to the boundaries of David's kingdom at its peak, and therefore

20. Alt, "System", pp. 16-21 (cited from p. 17) [=*KS*, vol. 1 pp. 195-200]; cf. Y. Kaufmann, *History of the Religion of Israel*, vol. 4 (Jerusalem 1947), pp. 384-386 [Hebrew]; Noth, *Josua*, p. 13; id., "Ueberlieferung", p. 162; id., *History*, p. 54; Aharoni, *LB*, p. 234; Schmitt, *Frieden*, pp. 81-89; Wright, "Provinces", pp. 67*-68*.

the document must have been written in the days of the United Monarchy.[21]

3) The Purpose of the Boundary System

Two questions must now be asked: What was the purpose of the complete boundary system? What were the criteria for the inclusion of tribes within a scheme compiled in the time of the United Monarchy?

Alt argued that the purpose of the original document was to define the tribal territories in order to prevent future disputes. This is only a partial answer. It is clear that even in the days of David the old tribal frameworks were still viable, and in numerous cases the writer delineated the actual domain of the individual tribes in very precise terms (e.g., Josh. 15:6-10; 16:1-3, 6-7; 17:7-9; 18:12-19; 19:10-14). However, the scheme of the entire land divided into tribal territories does not reflect

21. Aharoni's discussion of the boundary system is especially controversial. On the one hand, he accepted Alt's thesis of a premonarchial date for the original boundary delineations. On the other hand he realized that the external boundaries of Judah and Asher are identical to the borders of the United Monarchy in the time of David (Aharoni, *LB*, pp. 212-217, 231, 237-238). His solution of this obvious contradiction was simple: to regard these two sections as secondary, not belonging to the original tribal boundaries (ibid., p. 234; see Noth, *Josua*, pp. 114-119). However, it is hard to find textual support for this claim either in the description of Judah's border or in the delineation of the inheritance of Asher.

the scattered and fragmented character of tribal life. The allotments were in fact actual tribal territories augmented by neighbouring land, so dividing the overall area of the United Monarchy among the Israelite tribes. Alt's interpretation of the complete boundary system is therefore insufficient.

Aharoni suggested (a) that the boundary system originated from the league of six northern tribes (Benjamin, Ephraim, Manasseh, Zebulun, Asher and Naphtali); (b) that in its late form it represents the administrative division of the kingdom in the time of David into twelve units; and (c) that only late in Solomon's reign were these replaced by the system of twelve districts. In his words: "Since David depended upon the traditional tribal boundaries for his administrative division, it would appear that he made use of the border descriptions from the northern tribal alliance to which were added town lists from other tribes...".[22]

These suggestions are open to criticism. First, that the boundary descriptions originated from the league of the six northern tribes, is, as shown above, untenable. Second, the boundary delineations are quite different from the "traditional tribal boundaries" in both their scope and their internal divisions. The boundary system of the twelve tribes does not represent the exact tribal reality. It is rather the district system (1 Kings 4:7-19), in which the conquered Canaanite territories

22. Aharoni, *LB*, pp. 227-239, 267, 277; cf. Gottwald, *Tribes*, pp. 161, 183, 368-369.

were for the most part separated from the nuclear inheritances of the Israelite tribes, that is closer to the traditional tribal boundaries [see chapter 5 pp. 178-180, 195]. Third, established administrative systems are often very enduring, as Alt remarked in his epoch-making study: "Ordnungen, die am Boden eines Landes haften, zeigen ueberall in der Geschichte ein aeusserst zaehes Leben; selbst ein Wechsel der Bevoelkerung wirft sie kaum einmal geradezu ueber den Haufen, sondern bringt hoechstens vereinzelte Aenderungen an ihnen zustande".[23]

Aharoni suggested that Solomon's administrative division was different from that of his father. In my opinion, however, Solomon's entire kingdom was a direct continuation of David's kingdom, and this included its administration and district system.[24]

Gottwald, developing Aharoni's line of enquiry, suggests that the twelve Israelite tribes were in existence in the premonarchial period, and that following David's unification of the kingdom, the former Canaanite city-states were incorporated in the twelve tribes, which then became his administrative districts. According to Gottwald, the twelve tribes of Josh. 13-19 were artificial units based to a certain

23. Alt, "Landnahme", p. 2 [=*KS,* vol. 1, p. 90]; cf. id., "Provinzen", pp. 229-234 [=*KS,* vol. 2, pp. 195-199].

24. This assumption was noted by Alt ("Staatenbildung", *KS,* vol. 2, pp. 51-52; "Stadtstaat", p. 15 [=*KS,* vol. 3, pp. 265-266]) and adopted by Mazar ("Dan", p. 71).

extent on the arbitrary attachment of Canaanite cities to the tribal inheritances. In his view, the boundary system was designed to define the new districts, and was later supplanted by Solomon's district system.[25]

The arguments against Aharoni's suggestions are equally valid with regard to Gottwald's. In addition, the latter's theory about a premonarchial loose confederation of twelve tribes which David recast into a system, is untenable. It is clear, both from texts and from archaeology, that premonarchial Israelite settlement was considerably more limited, both in area and in population, than David's kingdom. Also, Gottwald's assertion that the list represents a unified system and was drawn up for official purposes, cannot be accepted, in view of the differing descriptions within the boundary system and the schematic delineations of the former Canaanite parts of the tribal allotments. And finally, his claim that the district system replaced the boundary system is contradicted by a comparison of the two [see chapter 5 p. 195].

The present writer agrees with Kallai both as to the date and to the literary and ideological background of the tribal allotments. However, Kallai maintains that the boundary system included only ten tribes, Simeon and Dan having no part in it. He also rejects the idea that the border descriptions were a combination of reality and invention, emphasizes the

25. Gottwald, *Tribes*, pp. 366-375.

authentic foundation of all ten tribal boundaries, and tries to find an administrative background for the system.[26]

As noted above, Alt pointed out that several inheritances within the boundary system were not genuine tribal territories, but a combination of tribal nuclear areas and additional – sometimes extensive – adjacent regions. This observation was made in connection with his suggestion concerning claims of the tribes to the neighbouring Canaanite areas of the premonarchial period, which has already been rejected above. But our objection to the early dating of the boundary system does not invalidate Alt's other proposition, that the nuclear tribal areas were systematically enlarged by including the adjacent Canaanite territories in order to divide the entire area west of the Jordan among the tribes of Israel.

26. Kallai, "Town Lists", pp. 135-137; id., *Tribes, passim;* id., "Frameworks"; id., "United Monarchy". In addition to the boundary system and the district system, Kallai (*Tribes*, pp. 379-389; "Frameworks", pp. 216-217; "System", pp. 22-25) has also dated the system of Levitical cities to the time of the United Monarchy, regarding all three systems as administrative structures within the Israelite kingdom. He is not clear about the specific role of each of these within the kingdom, and his claim of three parallel systems serving simultaneously within the confines of a single kingdom is not convincing. In chapter 6 we try to demonstrate that the complete system of Levitical cities is entirely non-historical and never served as an administrative structure. For the historicity of the boundary system, see below, pp. 98-102.

All the western parts of the internal boundaries, i.e., between tribes, were described briefly in a schematic manner which is in sharp contrast to the detailed description of the sections in the east. This applies to the western part of Ephraim's southern border (Josh. 16:3, 6); the boundary between Ephraim and Manasseh (Josh. 16:8; 17:9); the western border of Zebulun (Josh. 19:11, 14) and the southern border of Asher (Josh. 19:25-26). It is only the western external boundaries of the United Monarchy – those with the kingdoms of Philistia (Josh. 15:10b-11), the enclave of Joppa (Josh. 19:46) and the kingdoms of Sidon and Tyre (Josh. 19:28b-29) – that are described in detail. The boundary between the inheritances of Manasseh and its northern neighbours Asher and Issachar is vague, being indicated only by the names of towns (Josh. 17:11; 19:17-21). Furthermore, the northern part of the border between the inheritances of Asher and Naphtali is hardly described at all (Josh. 19:28a, 34b).

The borders delineated in this schematic, sometimes even obscure, manner have a common factor: they all passed through territories which were not conquered until the time of David. We may therefore conclude that it is only the genuine nuclear tribal inheritances and the external boundaries of the Israelite kingdom that were described in detail. The former Canaanite areas, having nothing to do with the tribal reality, served only as additions to and completions of the authentic tribal areas to fill the gap between them and the borders of the Israelite kingdom.

A further indication of the influence of theoretical considerations on the design of the boundary system is to be found in an analysis of the territory of the northern half of Dan. An examination of the boundary system shows that Naphtali's northern boundary is missing (Josh. 19:34) and that there is a gap between its inheritance and the northern limit of the borders of the tribes west of the Jordan [see chapter 1 p. 46]. This gap may be explained by the assumption that the author of the tribal allotments had included a territory for Dan in the central area, and was therefore obliged to ignore its northern half. He could neither assign the well-defined northern Danite territory to the tribe of Naphtali nor ascribe a city named Dan to Naphtali. Therefore he disregarded the northern Danite inheritance altogether, thus creating a gap.[27]

27. Noth ("Studien", pp. 227-228; *Josua*, pp. 14, 77, 120-123) proposed that the northern half of the tribe of Dan was included within the original document of the boundary delineations, and that it was subsequently replaced by the southern half of Dan, which was artificially inserted in place of the western extension of Benjamin's inheritance. According to this hypothesis, the gap in the north was created by the intervention of a late redactor. The theory, however, presents many problems. The entire reconstruction rests on two assumptions – the original inclusion of the northern Danite inheritance within the boundary system and the original extension of Benjamin's borders to the Mediterranean – both lacking textual support. Furthermore, Noth's suggestion that Josh. 19:33 described Naphtali's northern border ("Studien", pp. 225-227; *Josua*, pp. 119-120) is certainly wrong: the verse delineated the southern border of Naphtali (Aharoni, *LB*, p. 238, with further literature in n. 163; Kallai,

Finally, we may note the inclusion of the coast of Philistia within the inheritance of Judah. This inclusion is remarkable, since all other borders of the boundary system reflect the confines of David's kingdom at its zenith and exclude the territories of the neighbouring vassal kingdoms (Tyre, Sidon, Aram, Ammon, Moab, Edom). The attachment of the kingdoms of the Philistines to Judah's allotment was explained above as a result of the bias of the author of the system [chapter 1 pp. 64-66]. This is yet another instance of his tendency to include in the system theoretical rather than actual situations.

We have now established that the boundary system, dividing the entire Israelite kingdom into tribal allotments, was comprised of tribal as well as non-tribal regions, combined according to a careful plan.

Was there any specific administrative need for such a system? The answer to this crucial question is, in my opinion, no. The boundary system is a historiographic composition based on reality both in its outer limits and in parts of its internal borders. Once we classify the composition as historiographic

Tribes, pp. 193-195). The absence of Naphtali's northern border does not suit Noth's theory, according to which only Dan's northern inheritance should have been removed from the text. It is, rather, the northern part of Naphtali's allotment, and not the allotment of Dan, which was ignored in the boundary system. See also chapter 1 pp. 46-47 note 9.

and not administrative, we must try to explain it in the light of the literary and ideological climate at the time of the United Monarchy. The answer may be found in the concept that the 'twelve tribes of Israel' embodies the whole Israelite nation and symbolizes its unity. That is why the tribes are so prominent in the descriptions of the conquest and the settlement in the book of Joshua. Moreover, the motif of conquest served to legitimize the Israelite hold on David's new territories. Thus, the concept of the twelve-tribe system is inseparable from the historiographic motif of occupation and settlement, in both an ideological and a literary sense.

The concept of twelve tribes seems to have taken shape in the time of the United Monarchy. Thereafter it is a major element in biblical historiographic compositions.[28] Was it a reality or was it formulated purely for historiographic purposes?[29] One would expect to find some evidence of the concept, so prominent in biblical historiography, in the actual

28. S. Mowinckel, " 'Rahelstaemme' und 'Leastaemme' ", in: *Von Ugarit nach Qumran, Festschrift O. Eissfeldt*, eds., J. Hempel und L. Rost (Berlin 1958), pp. 129-150; S. Herrmann, "Das Werden Israels", *ThLZ*, vol. 87 (1962), pp. 561-574; id., "Autonome Entwicklungen in den Koenigreichen Israel und Juda", *SVT*, vol. 17 (1968), pp. 139-158; O. Eissfeldt, "The Hebrew Kingdom", *The Cambridge Ancient History*, vol. II/2, third edition (Cambridge 1975), pp. 548-553; de Geus, *Tribes*, pp. 112-118, 211.

29. For an extensive discussion of the problem, see de Geus, *Tribes*, pp. 111-119, with further literature.

history of the people of Israel. Unfortunately, no such evidence is traceable, unlike 'Israel' and 'Judah', which were realities in both the premonarchial and United Monarchy periods.[30] The complicated nature of the problem can be gathered from the following example.

In a survey of the area covered by the inheritance of Issachar, Gal was able to demonstrate that the main period of settlement was in the 10th century B.C., and that most of the sites were later abandoned. From this we may infer: (a) that Issachar settled in his inheritance at a relatively late date; (b) that the long list of towns of Issachar (Josh. 19:17-22) must be assigned to the 10th century B.C., i.e., the United Monarchy; (c) that some families of Issachar originally settled in Manasseh, and only later migrated to their new territories; and (d) that some families of Issachar remained in the territory of Manasseh.[31] It is also plausible that the clans who settled in

30. This is contrary to the conclusion of Kallai ("Judah and Israel – A Study in Israelite Historiography", *IEJ*, vol. 28 (1978), pp. 251-261). He suggests there that the distinctive designations of 'Judah' and 'Israel' and the concept of the ten tribes were all produced during the reign of David in Hebron and Eshbaal in Mahanaim. Basic problems, such as the rebellions of Absalom and Sheba or the appearance of Judah and Israel as two entities in the description of the reign of Saul (1 Sam. 11:8; 15:4; 17:52; 18:16), are ignored in his study. The complex nature of the problem calls for a far more extensive discussion.

31. Gal, *Issachar*, pp. 88-98; id., "The Settlement of Issachar: Some New Observations", *Tel Aviv*, vol. 9 (1982), pp. 79-86; cf.

the territory called Issachar may have consisted of families from different tribes. Therefore when the tribe of Issachar is mentioned in biblical historiography, we have to ask which area and which group is being referred to.

Anthropological and historical research has shown the flexibility of tribal structures, with a continuous disintegration and coalescence of splinter groups leaving one tribe for another, and constant fluctuations in size according to economic conditions.[32] The same is true of the Israelite settlement, with clans and families shifting from one place to another and integrating with their new neighbours, resulting in a number of discrepancies between the boundary system and the genealogical lists of the tribes.[33]

Herrmann, "Issakar", pp. 23-25, with further literature. The results of the survey definitely contradict Alt's view ("Galilaeische Ortsliste", pp. 73-81) that the town list of Issachar should be dated to the 7th century B.C.

32. M.B. Rowton, "Dimorphic Structure and the Problem of the *'apiru-'ibrim", JNES,* vol. 35 (1976), pp. 13-20; id., "Dimorphic Structure and the Tribal Elite", in: *al-Bahit, Festschrift J. Henninger zum 70 Geburtstag,* Studia Instituti Anthropos, vol. 28 (St. Augustin bei Bonn 1976), pp. 219-257; id., "Dimorphic Structure and the Parasocial Element", *JNES,* vol. 36 (1977), pp. 181-190; cf. M.D. Sahlins, *Tribesmen* (Englewood Cliffs, New Jersy 1968), *passim.*

33. J. Liver, "The Israelite Tribes", in: Mazar, *Judges,* pp. 204-211; Aharoni, *LB,* pp. 221-227; de Vaux, *Early History,* pp. 775-789.

In light of the above, the historicity of the system of the twelve tribes is inevitably enigmatic. It is probable that the concept of twelve tribes was coined only for the purpose of historiography, subsequently becoming a pivot for all accounts of the history of early Israel.

We have attempted to demonstrate that the system of the tribal allotments was a literary creation conceived during the United Monarchy and not an actual administrative division. This being so, the author was bound only by the framework he chose for his composition, dividing the whole country into twelve, according to the twelve tribe concept in vogue at that time.

4) The List of the Unconquered Canaanite Cities

The list of the unconquered Canaanite cities in Judg. 1:21, 27-35 (parts of which appear in Josh. 15:63; 16:10; 17:11-13) refers to them in connection with seven tribes: Benjamin, Ephraim, Manasseh, Zebulun, Asher, Naphtali and Dan. It is often argued that the cities that follow the mention of Dan (Judg. 1:34-35) really belonged to the House of Joseph, and that the list therefore pertains only to the inheritances of six tribes. Since this list corresponds in both outlook and content to the boundary system, the absence of the three tribes of Simeon, Dan and Issachar – or the first two only – was sometimes regarded as confirmation of the claim that the original list of tribal allotments included only six to ten tribes.[34]

Judg. 1:21, 27-35 may be regarded as the list of the main Canaanite cities west of the Jordan conquered by David. It was formulated at the time of the United Monarchy, its author describing contemporary conquests as cities which had not been conquered in the past. This picture must be accurate, since the writer knew very well which places were added to the kingdom in his own time.[35]

34. Alt, "System", pp. 13-18 [=*KS,* vol. 1, pp. 193-197]; id., "Galilaeische Ortsliste", pp. 64-68; Mowinckel, *Quellen,* p. 23; id., *Tetrateuch,* pp. 17-23; Noth, *Josua,* pp. 77, 113, 116-117; Aharoni, *LB,* pp. 212-215; Kallai, *Tribes,* pp. 90-96; Mayes, op.cit., [note 18 above], pp. 72-73; de Geus, *Tribes,* pp. 80-81; de Vaux, *Early History,* pp. 729-730; R. Smend, "Das uneroberte Land", in: Strecker, *Das Land,* pp. 91-102 (esp., pp. 100-101); Schmitt, *Frieden,* pp. 53-80 and further literature on p. 67 n. 53.

35. This explanation for the list of the unconquered Canaanite cities is closely related to the interpretations offered by Mowinckel (*Tetrateuch,* pp. 25-33) and by Kallai (*Tribes,* pp. 242-245). Gottwald (*Tribes,* pp. 167-175) suggested that the original "statement of accounts" of Judg. 1:21, 27-35 (ibid., p. 731 n. 116) was drawn up at the time of David's enthronment over all Israel, in order to define the tribal rights on these territories. The account was deposited in the state archives as a kind of witness to the entrenched tribalism in the new kingdom, thus compelling David to base and organize the new kingdom on the tribal-territorial lines. This theory lacks support or corroborative evidence, and its acceptability is a matter of personal choice.

The list of the unconquered Canaanite cities is actually a 'historical' document, formulated in this peculiar manner to serve the specific historiographic purpose of describing the conquest. Once this interpretation is accepted, it immediately becomes clear why several tribes are missing from the list. Since Transjordan was regarded as an area not belonging to Canaan, one would never expect to find the Transjordanian tribes in a list of unconquered Canaanite cities west of the Jordan.[36] The absence of Judah (and Simeon) could be explained by the desire of the writer, who was a Judaean, to make the point that only his own tribe was able to dispossess the Canaanites [see chapter 1 p. 65]. The reason for not including Issachar is different. Its territory contains only one main site, Tel Rekhesh (Tell el-Mukharkhash), which presumably was destroyed sometime during the 13th - 12th centuries B.C.[37] Thus, at the time of the United Monarchy no towns existed in Issachar to be included as points of reference in a list of unconquered cities. With regard to Dan, the list of Judg. 1 presupposes an inheritance of Dan in the Shephelah. Its position – after the three Galilean tribes – is the same as in the

36. De Vaux, *Early History*, pp. 128-133; cf. Schmitt, *Frieden*, pp. 65-66.

37. For Tel Rekhesh, see Y. Aharoni, "Anaharath", *JNES*, vol. 26 (1967), pp. 212-215; Gal, *Issachar*, pp. 33-40; id., "Tel Rekhesh", pp. 213-221. Other explanations were offered for the omission of Issachar from Judg. 1; see Taeubler, *Biblische Studien*, p. 115 n. 2; Mowinckel, *Tetrateuch*, pp. 24-25; Schmitt, *Frieden*, pp. 66-67, 82.

list of tribal allotments and other biblical tribal lists.[38] Although the list of unconquered Canaanite cities names only seven tribes, we may assume that the tribal boundaries included all twelve tribes.

5) David's Census and the Boundary System

An important question largely ignored in previous studies should now be considered: Why did the author of the boundary system use so many different devices? The lot of Simeon is the only one defined exclusively by a detailed list of towns. The lots of Dan and Issachar are described mainly by town lists, but each has also one border description. The inheritance of western Manasseh is indicated mainly by border lines, but its northern boundary is described by a list of towns. The descriptions of the Transjordanian and Galilean tribes have their particular characteristics. Of all the tribal inheritances, only Benjamin's is described in full in a counter-clockwise direction. Why could not the writer use one method to describe the whole system?[39]

38. Helga Weippert, "Das geographische System der Staemme Israels", *VT,* vol. 23 (1973), pp. 81, 86; K. Namiki, "Reconsideration of the Twelve Tribe System of Israel", *Annual of the Japanese Biblical Institute,* vol. 2 (1976), pp. 47-48, with further literature in n. 2.

39. Alt's clear-cut separation of boundary delineations and town lists minimizes the actual differences within the system. K.D. Schunck (*Benjamin: Untersuchungen zur Entstehung und Geschichte eines Israelitischen Stammes,* BZAW, vol. 86 (Berlin 1963), pp. 142-150) suggested that the different description devices are the result of the originally independent position of the tribal inheritances, which

The answer, in my opinion, must be sought in the sources from which the author of the system obtained all the details he needed – namely, David's census lists. What kind of records were written in the course of the census? Our main documentary evidence from the ancient Near East is the tablets of Mari, which supply a great deal of information about the compilation of the census lists in the kingdoms of Shamshi-Addu and Zimrilim.[40] These were written "place by place" and "name by name", and were used mainly for military purposes, and possibly for the corvée. Occasionally they were connected with the allotment of land and the examination of ownership rights on fields.

Unfortunately in 2 Sam 24 David's words in verse 2 do not specify the purpose of his census, though military service is implied in verse 9. Another census is described in Num. 26, where the actual count is followed by the words "To these

were combined only in later times. However, the unity of the boundary system and the harmonious standing of the single allotments are at variance with this theory.

40. J.R. Kupper, "Le recensement dans les textes de Mari", in: *Studia Mariana*, ed., A. Parrot (Leiden 1950), pp. 99-110; id., *Les nomades en Mésopotamie au temps des rois de Mari* (Paris 1957), pp. 22-29; E.A. Speiser, "Census and Ritual Expiation in Mari and Israel", *BASOR*, no. 149 (1958), pp. 17-25 (=*Oriental and Biblical Studies*, eds., J.J. Finkelstein and M. Greenberg (Philadelphia 1967) pp. 171-186); G.E. Mendenhall, "The Census Lists of Numbers 1 and 26", *JBL*, vol. 77 (1958), pp. 52-59; Rowton, in: *al-Bahit* [see note 32 above], pp. 240-250.

the land shall be divided for inheritance according to the number of names." (v. 53). The allotment of land was considered an integral part of the census in this account, as it is in the tablets of Mari.

Baechli noted the tradition of Josh. 18:1-10, in which seven tribal committees were nominated to register the inheritances of the tribes, and interpreted the passage as referring to the process by which the *Grenzfixpunkte* were recorded.[41] However, the activities of these *Flurkomissionen* must be related to the census, the delineation of territories being only one part of that opperation.

A census had many uses: besides being a register for military service it was also the basis for labour conscription, for levying and collecting taxes, for the allotment of fields and the examination of land ownership rights. By inference,

41. Baechli, "Liste", pp. 11-14. H.E. von Waldow ("Social Responsibility and Social Structure in Early Israel", *CBQ,* vol. 32 (1970), pp. 191-194) has compared the allotment of land to the tribes in Josh. 18:1-10 with the allotment to the clans in Num. 26:52-56. In his opinion, both texts describe the premonarchial practice of apportioning the clan's territory by lot. The description of Num. 26 is closer to the historical truth than that of Josh. 18, since the recipients of the land were the clans and not the tribes. Contrary to von Waldow, it seems to me that in fact the two texts reflect the reality of the monarchial period. Both should be explained in conjunction with the census, i.e., the examination of ownership rights of tribes and clans to their territories.

one may suggest that one of the main purposes of David's census was the exact delineation of territories in order to establish ownership rights. And it was in those areas where there were ownership disputes between neighbouring tribes that their territory had to be accurately demarcated and fully described. That was why the author of the boundary system was able to delineate those particular borderlines in such detail (e.g., Josh. 15:6-10; 16:1-3, 6-7; 17:7-9; 18:12-19; 19:10-14). This would fit in very well with his main purpose, which was the proper allocation of the territories to the Israelite tribes. In regions where there were no demarcation problems, such as the recently conquered Canaanite area, presumably the censors recorded only towns and their inhabitants. This lack of precise delineation was an obstacle to the author of the boundary system. In the west, he resolved the problem by following the river-beds to the sea, which necessarily led to a schematic description of the borders. In the other areas, he was obliged to use a combination of towns and borders, and sometimes merely a town list. By analysing the type of descriptions in the boundary system, we can learn what kind of records were made during the census in different parts of the country.

We may conclude that the form of the boundary system is the direct result of the sources available to its author: the original records of David's census. The varying descriptions do not justify tearing it to pieces. It was the nature of the documents on which the system was based that dictated its final literary form.

Another conclusion is that no complete, independent document or literary text delineating the tribal borders ever existed before the boundary system was formulated. Noth's *Urtext* i.e., the systematic listing of the border points is in fact the original record of the census. The assumption that the writer of the boundary system obtained all the details he needed from the original census lists, disposes of most of the difficulties in Noth's rigid scheme of the *Grenzfixpunkte.*

The boundary system as a historical source should now be reappraised. Since it was directly based on the original census lists, it is an important source of information about the early days of the monarchy. It certainly reflects the territorial situation at that time. For example, it tells us which tribal areas were densely populated and which were sparsely inhabited. A meticulous boundary description shows that two adjacent tribes had a conflict over their boundaries. Schematic boundaries or town lists indicate areas devoid of Israelite settlements or only sparsely populated. The suggestion that the boundary system was a non-administrative document does not mean that it cannot be fully exploited for historical and geographical research.

6) The Construction of the Boundary System

The first boundary to be drawn was probably the northern border of Judah, its eastern section marking the border with Benjamin and its western section that with the kingdoms of Philistia. Judah's other borders were copied from the description of the Land of Canaan (Num. 34:3-5). Benjamin's borders were drawn later, by encircling the tribe's allotment. Benjamin's southern border was constructed from Judah's northern border. We learn this from two errors caused by the reversal of the border points.

(a) Josh. 18:15 "And the southern side begins at the outskirts of Kiriath-jearim; and the boundary goes *ymh* (westward)...".[42] There could not have been a western turn in Benjamin's southern border. The mistake was in copying Judah's northern border instead of reversing the points. Josh. 15:10a "and the boundary circles *ymh* (west of) Baalah (i.e., Kiriath-jearim)...". If Benjamin's southern border was indeed a reversal of Judah's northern border, the next toponym ought to be mount Ephron (Josh. 15:9), between Baalah and the Waters of Nephtoah. But it is not there. We would suggest

42. Scholars have usually regarded the directive word *ymh* (westward) as a mistake, and recommended omitting it altogether (e.g., Steuernagel, *Josua*, p. 224; Cooke, *Joshua*, p. 169). Noth ("Studien", pp. 190-192; *Josua*, pp. 110-111) put forward that *ymh* is a remnant of the descritpion of Judah's border in 15:8, which was copied by mistake when the redactor changed the order of description of Benjamin's southern border. Aharoni (*LB*, p. 234 n. 148) suggested that *ymh* is a remnant of the ancient boundary description for this segment, which originally contained only this general designation. Kallai (*Tribes*, pp. 113-114) proposed that at Kiriath-jearim the border turned in two opposite directions, westwards and eastwards, *ymh* designating the turn to the west. See Schmitt, "Bet-awen", pp. 40-42.

amending the MT of Josh. 18:15 to "and the boundary goes from there to [Mount] Ephron...".[43]

(b) A similar mistake occurred in Josh. 18:16a: "then the boundary goes down to the border of the mountain...". The writer of this verse, when changing the order of toponyms which he took from Josh. 15:8b, made a mechanical inversion, not realizing that he was starting from the Waters of Nephtoah, and not from the side (*ktp*) of the Jebusite (Josh. 15:8a). From the Waters of Nephtoah one ascends (!) the mountain.

After delineating the southern tribes, the author turned to the four northern ones, starting with Zebulun. Next came Issachar. His northern boundary was indicated partly by towns previously marked on Zebulun's southern border – Chesulloth (Josh. 19:18) and Daberath (Josh. 19:20 LXX^{B}) – and partly by a boundary description, continuing Zebulun's southern border from mount Tabor to the Jordan.[44] Then came Asher,

43. Cf. RSV; Noth, *Josua*, pp. 110-111.

44. Josh. 19:22 "the boundary also touches (*pg'*) Tabor, Shahazumah, and Beth-shemesh, and its boundary ends at the Jordan...". The other three border descriptions along this line between the Jordan and the Mediterranean, are all delineated by starting from a particular point, first going to the end in one direction, returning (*šwb*) and then going to the end in the opposite direction (Josh. 19:10-12, 24-27, 33-34). Issachar's northern border is the only exception among the Galilean tribes. Furthermore, the toponym *šḥṣwmh* is not only non-Semitic in its appearance, but is obviously

whose boundary description refers to Zebulun's allotment (Josh. 19:27). The last was Naphtali's inheritance, where the description refers to both Zebulun and Asher (Josh. 19:34).

The tribes in the centre of the country were the last to be dealt with. This is evident from Josh. 17:10b-11, where Manasseh's northern border was demarcated by reference to Asher and Issachar. The description of the House of Joseph's southern border (Josh. 16:1-3, 5)[45] is closely related, with minor additions and alterations, to the text of Benjamin's

corrupt, leaving no clues for reconstruction. In the light of the parallel descriptions of the other Galilean tribes, would one dare to correct *wšḥṣwmh* and read it as *wšb qdmh* (and turned eastward)?

45. Josh. 16:1 is certainly corrupt. See Steuernagel, *Josua,* pp. 214-216; Cooke, *Joshua,* pp. 153-154; Noth, *Josua,* pp. 96, 101; Kallai, *Tribes,* pp. 121-122. The LXX reflects *w'lh myryḥw,* and was often accepted as the better text. Cooke (ibid., p. 154), on the basis of LXX and the parallel in Josh. 18:12 proposed: "and it goeth up from Jericho into the hill country to the wilderness of Bethel". In the light of Josh. 13:32 *m'br lyrdn yryḥw mzrḥh* one may suggest reading here *myrdn yryḥw mzrḥh* (from the Jordan by Jericho on the east side), cf. Simons, "Structure", p. 213 n. 2. Josh. 16:1 may accordingly be rendered *myrdn yryḥw mzrḥh lmy yryḥw w'lh myryḥw bhr mdbrh byt 'l* (from the Jordan by Jericho on the east side unto the waters of Jericho and it goes up from Jericho through the hill country to the wilderness of Bethel).

northern border (Josh. 18:12-13).[46] Dan's inheritance must have been drawn after Ephraim's and Manasseh's, since his borders presuppose the demarcation of his three neighbours – Judah, Benjamin and Ephraim. It was only on Dan's western side that the border was entirely missing, and the author of the boundary system found it necessary to define it (Josh. 19:46).

The delineation of the Transjordanian tribes is independent of those west of the Jordan and there is no way of determining when they were drawn.

The order of composition suggested here accords with the arrangement of the Solomonic district system (1 Kings 4:7-19). The latter is arranged in four territorial blocs: the districts in the centre of the country (vv. 8-12); the Transjordanian districts (vv. 13-14); the northern districts (vv. 15-17); and the southern districts (vv. 18, 19b). See chapter 5 below.

The inheritance of Simeon (Josh. 19:1-9) requires comment. It is stated explicitly that the Simeonite territory was inside Judah's territory (Josh. 19:1, 9). On the other hand, it covers a specified area, mainly in the western Negeb.[47] The Simeonites were certainly mixed with the clans of Judah; but similar cases of tribal intermingling did not prevent the

46. For a detailed comparison of the boundaries of Benjamin and the House of Joseph, see Schmitt, "Bet-awen", pp. 42-51.

47. Na'aman, "Simeon".

writer from assigning to each a well-defined allotment.[48] It seems to me that the emphasis on the inclusion of the territory of Simeon within that of Judah resulted from the desire of the author of the boundary system, who certainly belonged to Judah, to make his own tribe's inheritance as large as possible. The same bias can be observed in several other traditions. Its effect on the border descriptions was discussed in chapter 1 pp. 62-66. While the borders of Judah were artificially extended by incorporating the inheritance of Simeon, the latter was a distinct entity within the boundary system. It may have been recorded in the system after the delineation of Judah, but this cannot be established.

7) The Inheritance of Dan and the Second Solomonic District

We may now re-examine the allotment of Dan (Josh. 19:40-46) in relation to the boundaries of its neighbours Benjamin, Judah and Ephraim. The basis for this re-examination will be, with two exceptions, the identifications for the town list proposed by Mazar.[49]

48. Judah's inheritance was first united by David and included various tribal groups, such as Calebites, Kenizzites, Jerahmeelites, Kenites, as well as elements of Levites (see de Vaux, *Early History*, pp. 523-550, 674-675). For further literature see note 33 above.

49. Mazar, "Dan". For the archaeological survey along the Aijalon river, see R. Gophna, "The Settlement in the Biblical Period" in: *The Western Basin of the Aijalon River*, ed. S. Marton (Tel Aviv 1969), pp. 75-88 [Hebrew]. The identification of the city of

Benjamin's western border, which is Dan's eastern border, is drawn from Beth-horon southward to Kiriath-jearim (Josh. 18:14). The actual borderline, however, would seem to have run along the western margins of the foothills, in an area where there were no settlements to mark the boundary.[50] Parallel to this line lie the eastern towns of Dan's allotment (Zorah, Eshtaol, Ir-shemesh, Shaalbim, Aijalon).

Judah's northern border ran from Beth-shemesh along the Sorek river (Wadi es-Sarar) to Timnah, passed through the northern side (*ktp*) of the territory of Ekron, and followed

Gibbethon with Tell Melat was first proposed by G. von Rad ("Das Reich Israel und die Philister", *PJb,* vol. 29 (1933), p. 38), and has been generally accepted. However, Tell Melat seems too small a site for such an important city as Gibbethon. Furthermore, Gibbethon is depicted on a relief of Sargon II (P.E. Botta and E. Flandin, *Monument de Ninive,* vol. 2 (Paris 1849; reprinted Osnabruck 1972), pl. 89) and a stream is clearly seen nearby (Ruth Jacoby, "City Descriptions in the Assyrien Reliefs", M.A. Thesis (Jerusalem 1976), p. 78). Since Tell Melat is far from any river, its identification with Gibbethon does not hold. One may possibly locate Gibbethon at Ras Abu Ḥamid, near what was the Israelite-Philistine border in the 9th-8th centuries B.C. See Schmitt, "Gat", pp. 107-109. Tell Melat may be identified with Eltekeh, although the identification of the latter at Tell esh-Shallaf is equally possible. See S. Timm, "Die territoriale Ausdehnung des Staates Israel zur Zeit der Omriden", *ZDPV,* vol. 96 (1980), pp. 34-35.

50. Kallai, *Tribes,* pp. 107-108.

the wadi westwards through several places (Shikkeron, mount Baalah, Jabneel), until reaching the sea (Josh. 15:11).[51] Cross and Wright have pointed out that the same towns – Beth-shemesh, Timnah, Ekron, Baalath – are mentioned both in the northern boundary of Judah and in the town list of Dan.[52]

51. Aharoni ("The Northern Boundary of Judah", *PEQ,* vol. 90 (1958), pp. 27-31) correctly delineated the northern border of Judah along the Sorek river, identifying the toponyms mentioned in Josh. 15:11 along this line. He further claimed (ibid., p. 30) that *ktp 'qrwn ṣpwnh* refers to the slope opposite the city, i.e., the southern slope of the Sorek river. This interpretation was criticized by Kallai ("Kateph - *ktp*", *IEJ,* vol. 15 (1965), pp. 177-179), who maintained that the phrase referred to the northern slope of the hill of Ekron. Kallai was thus obliged to draw the border near the city of Ekron, south of the Sorek river. However, the basic meaning of *ktp* is 'side' and not 'slope'. See E. Dhorme, "L'emploi métaphorique des noms de parties du corps en Hébreu et en Akkadien. V. Le tronc", *RB,* vol. 31 (1922), p. 219; A. Schwarzenbach, *Die geographische Terminologie im Hebraeischen des Alten Testamentes* (Leiden 1954), pp. 18-19, 157; N. Avigad, "The Second Tomb-Inscription of the Royal Steward", *IEJ,* vol. 5 (1955), p. 165; R.D. Haak, "The 'Shoulder' of the Temple", *VT,* vol. 33 (1983), pp. 271-278. The meaning of 'slope' is only derivative, and is not inherent in the word *ktp.* "The side of Ekron northward" refers to the boundary of the territory of the city of Ekron, along the Sorek river, where the northern boundary of Judah should be delineated.

52. Cross-Wright, "Boundary", p. 210; cf. Steuernagel, *Josua,* p. 209. Aharoni's emendation of the text of Josh. 19:43 "...Timnah, Ekron," to "Timnath-Ekron" (*LB,* pp. 266-267) seems redundant.

This is not exceptional; there are numerous other cases where the same toponyms appear in the border descriptions of neighbouring tribes. For example: Heshbon, which was a city of Reuben (Josh. 13:17), also appears as a border town of Gad (Josh. 13:26); Mahanaim, which was a city of Gad (Josh. 13:26), also appears as a border town of Manasseh (Josh. 13:30). Beth-shemesh appears both in the border description of Issachar (Josh. 19:22) and in the town list of Naphtali (Josh. 19:38). Chisloth-tabor and Daberath appear both in the border description of Zebulun and in the town list of Issachar.[53] Beth-hoglah and Beth-arabah appear both in the border descriptions of Judah (Josh. 15:6) and Benjamin (Josh. 18:18-19). One may suggest that the author of the boundary system selected several towns from the description of Judah's northern border in order to define Dan's southern border precisely.[54] Dan's town list thus includes border points as well as towns located in the interior of the inheritance.

Timnah was a well known place and no further indication was needed to specify its location. Ekron belonged to a series of four toponyms (the other three are Beth-shemesh, Timnah and Baalath) appearing both in the northern boundary of Judah and the town list of Dan, indicating the contiguity of the two borders.

53. Chisloth-tabor (Josh. 19:12) and Chesulloth (Josh. 19:18); Daberath (Josh. 19:12) and Rabbith (Josh. 19:20. LXX *Dabirōn*).

54. The border running westward from Timnah was actually that of the kingdom of David, which is why it was precisely defined in the boundary system.

Determining the northern border of Dan is more complicated. Ephraim's border ran from Beth-horon westwards to Gezer and the sea (Josh. 16:3, 5-6a). Several biblical passages refer to the settlement of Ephraimite families in the area around Gezer (Josh. 16:10; Judg. 1:29, 35; 1 Chr. 7:21, 28). The description of the border in Josh. 16:3 reflects the territorial expansion of Ephraim into the Shephelah. The actual line of Ephraim's border, running through the area recently conquered by David west of Upper Beth-horon (Josh. 16:5-6a) and Gezer (Josh. 16:3), is obscure.[55] But the missing parts can be looked for in Dan's town list (Josh. 19:42, 45). Shaalbim and Aijalon are situated east of Gezer, near the Aijalon river (Wadi el-Kabir); Jehud, Azor and Bene-berak[56] are all located along it, north-west of Gezer. Thus, the border between Ephraim and Dan must have run along the Aijalon river, by-passing the Ephraimite enclave around Gezer. Of the five points mentioned, Aijalon and Azor are on the south side of the border, the other three on the north side. The same is

55. Noth ("Studien", pp. 227-228; *Josua,* pp. 77, 120-123) suggested that the inheritance of Benjamin originally included that of Dan. Subsequently Benjamin's inheritance was cut in the west, in order to make space for Dan. This proposition was adopted by Aharoni (*LB,* pp. 229-230; 235-236). Kallai (*Tribes,* pp. 122-126) suggested that Dan's inheritance was included in Ephraim's. Thus according to both Noth and Kallai Dan had no place whatever in the boundary system. See also note 42 above.

56. LXX^B has Azor and Bene-berak; MT and LXX^A have Jehud and Bene-berak.

true of Dan's southern border, where the towns are located on both sides of the Sorek river.

Josh. 19:46 is a very fragmentary border description. With the aid of the LXX we may reconstruct its original text as follows: and on the west (*wmym*) was Jarkon, to (*'d*) the border over against Joppa.[57] The biblical Jarkon river is clearly the western part of the Aijalon river (Wadi el Barideh) running in a south-north direction.[58] Dan's western border ran along this wadi and then southwards, leaving Joppa out of the inheritance. The accurate delineation of Dan's western border is due to the fact that it was also the external boundary of the Israelite kingdom. In Josh. 15:10b-11 and 19:28b-29 the tribal border and external boundary coincide, and therefore all of these are described in detail.

Mazar's proposed location of Gath-rimmon at Tel Gerisa (Tell el-Jerisheh) is possible, though the latter site may have belonged to Ephraim.[59] Strange suggests that Gath-rimmon is Ras Abu Ḥamid,[60] which Mazar identifies as Gath or Gittaim,

57. Steuernagel, *Josua,* p. 230; Noth, *Josua,* p. 118; Cross-Wright, "boundary", p. 210; cf. Strange, "Dan", pp. 129-130.

58. Noth, *Josua,* p. 121.

59. Mazar, "Dan", pp. 67-70; but cf. id., "The Early Israelite Settlement in the Hill Country", *BASOR,* no. 241 (1981), p. 80.

60. Strange, "Dan", pp. 122-129; see also Schmitt, "Gat", pp. 115-131.

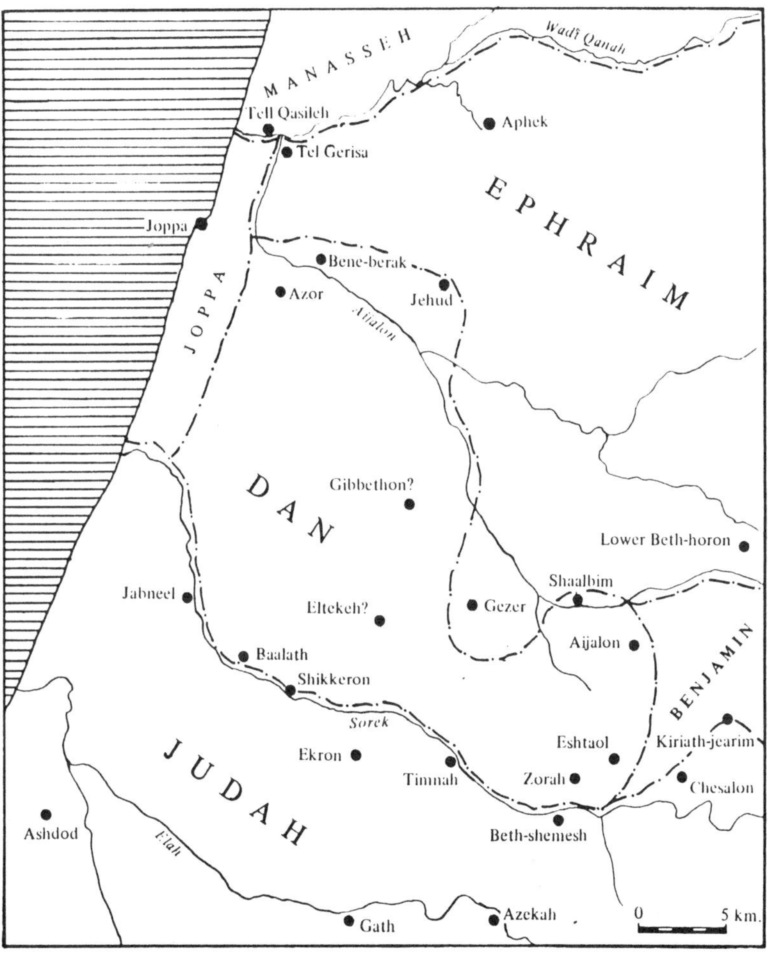

Map 3. Dan's Inheritance.

mentioned in biblical and post-biblical sources.[61] Strange's suggestion is possible but I would prefer to identify Ras Abu Ḥamid as Gibbethon [see above pp. 107-108, note 49].[62]

Further information about the inheritance of Dan can be gleaned from the second district of Solomon (1 Kings 4:9). As a result of a misinterpretation, the word *mqṣ* was regarded as a toponym (Makaz) prefixed by the preposition *b*. The toponym, however, is actually an abbreviation of the Hebrew word *mqṣ[h]* (from the end of), which is common in border descriptions (Josh. 15:2b; 18:15a).[63] The original text may

61. B. Mazar, "Gath and Gittaim", *IEJ,* vol. 4 (1954), pp. 227-235. The identification was accepted by Rainey ("The Identifiaction of Philistine Gath", *Eretz Israel,* vol. 12 (1975), pp. 63*-67*) and Avi-Yonah (*Gazetteer,* p. 62). For a comprehensive discussion of the problem, see Schmitt, "Gat", pp. 77-131.

62. The main obstacle to the identification of Gitta(m) at Ras Abu Ḥamid is the description of Eusebius (*Onomastikon,* paragraph 246, p. 72 lines 1-3), mentioning "a very large village, which is called Giththam as one goes from Antipatris to Jamnia". If Eusebius had had modern Ras Abu Ḥamid in mind, he would have given the distance from Diospolis and not from Antipatris. See G. Beyer, "Die Stadtgebiete von Diospolis und Nikopolis im 4 Jahrh. n. Chr. und ihre Grenznachbarn", *ZDPV,* vol. 56 (1933), pp. 227-228; A. Alt, "Gitthaim", *PJb,* vol. 35 (1939), p. 104 n. 2; Schmitt, "Gat", pp. 92-102.

63. The proposal to regard *mqṣ* as a common word and not as a toponym has already been suggested by F. Pintore ("Intendenti",

be reconstructed as follows: The son of Deker, from the end (*mqṣh*) of Shaalbim and Beth-shemesh and Aijalon to (LXX)[64] Beth-hanan". As already noted, Shaalbim was a border town of Ephraim; opposite it appears Beth-shemesh, which was a Judaean town (Josh. 15:10). Aijalon was situated on the western border of Dan, and Beth-hanan should be looked for in the opposite direction, roughly on the eastern border of the enclave of Joppa. The writers of both the Solomonic districts and the inheritance of Dan used border-towns of neighbouring tribes to indicate their limits. The main difference between the two systems is that Gezer and its vicinity, assigned to Ephraim in the boundary system, seems to have been included within the second Solomonic district.

One can get a better understanding of the second Solomonic district by comparing it with the fifth. The fifth district actually consists of Canaanite-occupied parts of the valleys of Jezreel and Beth-shean, which in the boundary system

p. 190). His explanation however, is not convincing. First, the reconstructed form *bmqṣw* does not appear elsewhere in the Bible. Secondly, the proposed use of this word, as referring to the previously-mentioned district of Mount Ephraim, has no parallel in the list. Each district is described independently.

64. C.F. Burney, *Notes on the Hebrew Text of the Books of Kings* (Oxford 1903; reprinted New York 1970), p. 41; A. Šanda, *Die Buecher der Koenige Uebersetzt und Erklaert, Exegetisches Handbuch zum Alten Testament,* vol. 1 (Muenster 1911), pp. 75-76.

(Josh. 17:11) were allotted to Manasseh [see pp. 187-190]. The similarity between the second and fifth districts is obvious: both were Canaanite districts conquered and annexed to the kingdom of Israel in the days of David. That is why they were both described in the boundary system by a list of towns. The writer of the district system found this method unsuitable for his purposes and used a different one.

The boundary system has been presented above as a combination of nuclear tribal areas and additional Canaanite regions. What does 'the inheritance of Dan' really mean? It is evident from the Bible that clans of Dan settled in the Shephelah, west of the Judaean hills, in the region of Zorah and Eshtaol. Some families remained on the eastern fringes of the Shephelah even after part of the tribe had migrated northwards as a result of the encroachment of the Philistines and the indigenous population.[65] This is reflected in the stories of Samson (Judg. 13-16). Most of the Danite allotment remained outside the Israelite domain until David's time. The author of the boundary system, in order to achieve his basic purpose – the division of the entire land among the twelve tribes – assigned the recently-conquered district to the nearest families, which happened to belong to the tribe of Dan. This was not an unusual practice when dividing the tribal allotments.

65. These inhabitants were called Amorites (Josh. 19:47-48 LXX; Judg. 1:34). See S. Holmes, *Joshua, the Hebrew and Greek Texts* (Cambridge 1914), pp. 14-16, 70-71; A.G. Auld, "Judges I and History: A Reconsideration", *VT,* vol. 25 (1975), pp. 277-278.

For example, while the tribe of Asher was located mainly on the hills of western Galilee, the author also assigned it the northern coastal plain, from the Kishon to the Litani. In the same way, the valleys of Jezreel and Beth-shean and the northern plain of Sharon (Dor), recently conquered by David, were allotted to Manasseh, whose territory was nearest. The recently-conquered areas in Transjordan were divided among the three tribes, Reuben, Gad and Manasseh. One may conclude that it is only by combining the tribal reality, the political situation in the time of the United Monarchy and the historiographic objectives of the writers, that the tribal allotments of Joshua 13-19 can be fully understood and historically exploited.

CHAPTER THREE

MAROM / MARON AND THE BOUNDARY BETWEEN ZEBULUN AND NAPHTALI

The location of the Canaanite city of Madon (Josh. 11:1; 12:19) and of the waters of Merom, where Joshua defeated a league of Canaanite kings (Josh. 11:5, 7), has been disputed ever since the early days of modern historical research. Many scholars have pointed out the phonetic resemblance of Madon and Khirbet Madin (a small site on the northern flank of Tel Qarnei Hittin), and identified the biblical city with the nearby Tel Qarnei Hittin (Qarn Ḥaṭṭin) in Lower Galilee. They then placed the waters of Merom in Upper Galilee, near the village of Meron, at the foot of Jebel Jermaq.[1] Others regarded both

1. For the identification of biblical Madon with Tel Qarnei Hittin, see the extensive literature in T.L. Thompson, *The Settlement of Palestine in the Bronze Age,* Beiheft TAVO, Reihe B, vol. 34 (Wiesbaden 1979), p. 107. For the identification of the waters of Merom with the spring of Meiron, see W.F. Albright, "New Israelite and Pre-Israelite Sites: The Spring Trip of 1929", *BASOR,* no. 35 (1929), pp. 8-9; Abel, *Géographie,* p. 385; cf. Roesel, "Kriege", pp. 179-181.

names as textual variations,[2] and therefore sought only one location. They placed the city either near the village of Marun er-Ras, at the foot of Jebel Marun, or at Tell el-Khirbeh (map reference 190.275), near the village of Yarun, identifying the spring gushing near the site as the waters of Merom.[3] These identifications have been discussed in great detail by Roesel,[4] and we shall therefore confine ourselves to our own arguments for the location of Maron and the waters of Merom.

We suggest that (a) the very similar names of Marom and Maron refer to the same Canaanite city; (b) that this city was situated at Tel Qarnei Hittin; and (c) that it was mentioned not only in the conquest tradition of Joshua but also in the description of the eastern border of the inheritance of Zebulun and in the list of Levitical cities of Zebulun.

2. Reading Maron as in the LXX of Josh. 11:1. In Josh. 12:20 LXX also has "the king of Shim'on the king of Maron" instead of the king of Shimron-meron.

3. For the identification of the waters of Merom and the city of Maron near the village of Marun er-Ras, see W. Gover, "The Waters of Merom", *PEF QSt,* 1890, pp. 50-54; J. Garstang, *Joshua Judges* (London 1931), pp. 187-195, 393. For the identification of Maron with Tell el-Khirbeh, see Aharoni, *Settlement,* pp. 95-98; id., *LB,* pp. 106, 206, 210.

4. Roesel, "Kriege", pp. 171-183.

1) The Original Name of the City

In Josh. 11:1 the city ruled by Jobab is called mdwn in MT and LXX^A, and *mrwn* in LXX^B. It would seem to me that by following LXX^B, as several scholars have suggested, a few advantages are to be gained. (a) We can identify Maron with the waters of Merom, the site of the battle in verse 5. (b) The original name of this Canaanite city was probably Marom, meaning height, a name common in the toponymic tradition of the second millennium B.C.[5] (c) The ending of the name *–on* is nothing but a byform, an exchange for *–om*, the common Semitic suffix.[6] (d) The name Maron appears also in Josh. 12:20, where MT has the meaningless "the king of *šmrwn*

5. M. Noth, "Die Wege der Pharaonenheere in Palaestina und Syrien, Teil V: Ramses II in Syrien", *ZDPV*, vol. 64 (1941), p. 59 n. 1 [=*Aufsaetze*, vol. 2, p. 107 n. 77]; Borée, *Ortsnamen*, p. 72.

6. The interchange of the endings *m* and *n* is often found in Galilean toponyms of the Roman and Byzantine periods, e.g., Nimrim – Nimrin; Sochim – Sochin; Sapphorim – Sapphorin (for Sepphoris). Cf. S. Klein, *Beitraege zur Geographie und Geschichte Galilaeas* (Leipzig 1909), *passim*. This alteration is common, e.g., Kiriathaim (Num. 32:37; Josh. 13:19) - Kiriaten (the Mesha Stele, line 10); Shaalbim (Judg. 1:35; 1 Kings 4:9) - Shaalabbin (Josh. 19:42); Gershom (1 Chr. 6:16, 17, 43, 62, 71 [= MT 6:1, 2, 28, 47, 56]) – Gershon (Gen. 46:11; Ex. 6:16; 1 Chr. 6:1 [=MT 5:27]); *hyklym* (Thutmes III) – *hyklyn* (Amenhotep III); *'trn* (Amenhotep II) – *'drm* (Shishak).

mr'wn",[7] and one should follow the LXX "the king of Shim'on, the king of Maron...". A city named Madon is not known from any other document, and it may be regarded as a scribal error. It would accordingly follow that one has to discard the location of Khirbet Madin.

2) The Battle at the Waters of Merom and the Site of Marom/ Maron

The descriptions of the conquest of northern Canaan in Josh. 11 and of southern Canaan in Josh. 10 share the same historiographic aims and ideology, and there are certain similarities in their general outlines.[8] The two stories were part of a pre-Deuteronomistic composition, probably dating from the time of the United Monarchy. This described the conquest of the area covered by the inheritances of the Israelite tribes, i.e., the Israelite kingdom at its apogee at the end of David's reign. The conquest of the south was related as starting in the centre of the land, in the Jerusalem area, where the decisive battle was fought, and reaching the extreme southern border-point of Kadesh-barnea (Josh. 10:41). As will be shown, the conquest of the north was recounted in a similar manner. It started at the southern border of the Galilean tribes, where the decisive battle was fought, and reached their extreme northern border. See chapter 1, pp. 48-50.

7. A. F. Rainey, "Toponymic Problems: Shim'on - Shimron", *Tel Aviv*, vol. 3 (1976), p. 57; cf. Weippert, *Settlement*, p. 35 n. 101.

8. Noth, *Josua*, p. 67; de Vaux, *Early History*, p. 655.

When one examines the composition of the northern Canaanite league in Josh. 11:1, the location of Marom / Maron is obvious. Hazor, whose king was leader of the allies, lay to the south of lake Huleh; Shim'on (MT Shimron) is commonly identified with Khirbet Sammuniyeh; [9] Achshaph was situated in the plain of Acco, possibly at Tell Kisan.[10] One would expect Marom / Maron to connect Hazor on the one side, with Shim'on and Achshaph on the other. There is only one site which would fulfil this requirement and which archaeologically fits a Canaanite city, and that is Tel Qarnei Hittin. This is a rocky, high mound, strategically placed on the main road connecting the Jordan valley with Lower Galilee and the Jezreel and Acco plains.[11] An experimental dig showed that the site was fortified on its southern summit during the 14th-13th centuries B.C. and again in Iron Age II. Pottery from Iron Age I was also recovered.[12] In LB II Marom / Maron had

9. See Rainey, op. cit. [note 7 above], pp. 57-69; id., "Shimron", *EM*, vol. 8 (1982), pp. 140-142 [Hebrew], with further literature.

10. See Weippert, *Settlement*, pp. 35-36 n. 102, with further literature; J. Briend, "Akshaph et sa localisation à Tell Keisan", RB, vol. 79 (1972), pp. 239-246; P. Bordreuil, "De 'Arqa à Akshaph: Notes de toponymie phênicienne", in: *La Toponymie Antique* (Actes du Colloque de Strasbourg, 12-14 Juin 1975), Université des Sciences Humaines de Strasbourg, pp. 180-184.

11. Aharoni, "Remarks", p. 180; Gal, "Tel Rekhesh", p. 215.

12. Gal, "Tel Rekhesh", pp. 215-218; cf. Thompson, op. cit. [note 1 above], p. 107.

apparently been a small independent city-state, bordering in the east on the strong kingdom of Hazor, which controlled the entire northern Jordan valley up to the Yarmuk river, and in the west on the kingdom of Shim'on.[13] Whether it was mentioned in the Egyptian topographical lists of the second millennium cannot yet be decided.[14] The city was probably destroyed some time during the 13th century B.C. and was sparsely settled by the Israelites in the 12th-11th centuries.

Significant support for the location of Marom / Maron in Lower Galilee is provided by the annals of Tiglath-pileser III.[15] The passage about the conquest of the kingdom of Israel by

13. The extensive territory of the kingdom of Hazor is reflected in an Amarna letter (EA 364) in which the king of Hazor is accused of capturing towns of the king of Ashtaroth. The towns (or rather, villages) must have been situated in the area of the Yarmuk river, since the Golan Heights, east of Hazor, were not occupied in the second millennium B.C. See A.F. Rainey, *El Amarna Tablets 359-379,* AOAT, vol. 8, second edition (Neukirchen-Vluyn 1978), pp. 26-27, with further literature; Na'aman, "Amarna", pp. 50-54.

14. Roesel, "Kriege", pp. 177-178, with further literature.

15. P. Rost, *Die Keilschrifttexte Tiglath-Pileser III* (Leipzig 1893), p. 38 lines 229-234 and pls. XVIIIa and XVIIIb; Forrer, *Provinz,* pp. 60-61. The definitive publication, based on the original handwriting of H. Layard, is that of H. Tadmor, "The Conquest of Galilee by Tiglath Pileser III, King of Assyria", in: *All the Land of Naphtali,* ed. H.Z. Hirschberg, (the Twenty-Fourth Archaeological Convention, Jerusalem 1967), pp. 63-64 [Hebrew].

the Assyrian king was only partially preserved in two fragments dealing with the end of the campaign. The text begins with a summary of the preceding section, which may be reconstructed as follows:[16] "[I razed to the gr]ou[nd xx cities] of the 16 districts of the Land of Bit [Humri]". Then comes a list of cities accompanied by the number of deportees taken from each place and the text ends with a statement which may tentatively be restored:[17] "[I had them cross] difficult mountains [and brought them to the Land of...]".

The names of many cities were either lost or poorly preserved, but the four towns that can be identified are all situated in a well-defined area, the inheritance of Zebulun. They are Ḫinnatuna (Hannathon), Yaṭbite (Joṭbah), Aruma (Rumah) and Marum (Marom). Aruma / Rumah is undoubtedly identical with Ruma of the Roman and Byzantine periods, today Khirbet er-Rumeh (map reference 177.243), on the south side of the Beth-netophah valley (Sahl el-Baṭṭof).[18] Marum / Marom, which is mentioned next, tallies perfectly with Tel Qarnei Hittin, five km. east of the valley, on roughly the same latitude as Rumah.

16. Rost, ibid., pl. XVIIIa line 3 and pl. XVIIIb line 2.

17. Rost, ibid., pl. XVIIIa line 11. For the restoration cf. ibid., p. 80 lines 16-17.

18. Avi-Yonah, *Gazetteer*, p. 91; A.F. Rainey, "Rumah", *EM*, vol. 7 (1976), p. 337 [Hebrew], with further literature.

The ancient name of Marom / Maron may have survived in the nearby village of Nimrin, three km. west of Tel Qarnei Hittin, which was known in the Roman period as Kfar Nimrah.[19] Nimrah may be considered as a metathesis of Maron, which was associated with the leopard (*nmr*), the name only being attached to the site long after it was destroyed. This is no more than a theory; the identification of the site is not dependent on the preservation of the name.

The Waters of Merom are most probably the spring of Wadi el-Ḥamam north of Tel Qarnei Hittin. The topographical background of the story of Josh. 11 may therefore be analysed as follows: (a) The four Canaanite kingdoms of Hazor, Marom, Shim'on and Achshaph, situated along the borders of Galilee, were deliberately used by the writer to demonstrate that it only required a single victory over their league to conquer the whole region. The site of the decisive battle was placed on the main route leading to Hazor, "...the head of all those kingdoms" (Josh. 11:10). (b) The conquest of the entire Galilee ostensibly developed in three stages: (1) Victory in one decisive battle. (2) Pursuit of the retreating enemy as far as Sidon the Great, Misrephoth-maim and the valley of Mizpeh, which all lay in a west-east line along the northern boundary of the Israelite tribal inheritances. (3) Capture and destruction of the leading city of Hazor.

19. Klein, *Galilee, passim;* Avi-Yonah, *Gazetteer,* p. 73.

We may conclude that the story was constructed in a sophisticated manner to serve a double historiographic purpose: to show how the northern parts of the tribal allotments came into the possession of the Israelite tribes, and to legitimize that possession by claiming that it had been in Israelite hands since the time of Joshua. The historicity of the story as a whole, or of its individual episodes, remains open to question.

3) Shemesh-edom and Adamah

The proposed location of Marom/Maron at Tel Qarnei Hittin negates Aharoni's identification of this site as Shemesh-edom mentioned in the Egyptian sources and as biblical Adamah of the inheritance of Naphtali (Josh. 19:36).[20]

Shemesh-edom is mentioned twice: first in the topographical list of Thutmes III and secondly in the stelae of Amenhotep II describing the campaign of his seventh year. Two quite different locations have been suggested for the city. Edel,[21] followed by Helck,[22] proposed a site north of the

20. Y. Aharoni, "The Land of 'Amqi", *IEJ,* vol. 3 (1953), p. 157 n. 22; id., "Remarks", pp. 177-181.

21. Edel, "Stelen", pp. 146-147.

22. Helck, *Beziehungen,* p. 131; cf. A.H. Gardiner, *Ancient Egyptian Onomastica,* vol. 1 (Oxford 1947), pp. 163-166; S. Smith, *The Statue of Idri-mi* (London 1949), pp. 50-51; Weippert, *Settlement,* p. 34 n. 100.

borders of Canaan, while Aharoni located it at Tel Qarnei Hittin, in Lower Galilee.[23] The enormous distance between the locations is the result of a different interpretation of the sources.

Aharoni based his arguments on the fact that Shemesh-edom precedes Anaharath in the topographical list of Thutmes III (nos. 51-52). Since Anaharath belongs to the inheritance of Issachar (Josh. 19:19), he located Shemesh-edom in the same area, viz., Lower Galilee. However, it was Aharoni himself who had argued convincingly that the list was arranged according to geographical regions. Therefore the entire section in which Shemesh-edom was included (nos. 48-59) needs to be considered.

The first site of this section *rš qdš* (no. 48) should be located in northern Canaan, as is evident from its appearance in another topographical list, that of Ramesses II.[24] The two

23. Aharoni's identification of Shemesh-edom with Tel Qarnei Hittin was accepted by Gal ("Tel Rekhesh", p. 221) and Weinstein ("The Egyptian Empire in Palestine: A Reassessment", *BASOR,* no. 241 (1981), p. 13). S. Aḥituv ("The Egyptian Topographical Lists Relating to the History of Palestine in the Biblical Period", Ph.D. Thesis, Hebrew University Jerusalem 1979, pp. 182-186 [Hebrew]) accepted Aharoni's argumentation in general. Nevertheless, he proposed to locate Adumim of Thutmes' list (no. 36) at Tel Qarnei Hittin, placing Shemesh-edom at el-'Abeidiyeh, 15 km. south-east of Tel Qarnei Hittin.

24. See Helck, *Beziehungen,* p. 209, II no. 1, with further literature.

towns of Ḫašhabu (no. 55) and Tushulti (no. 56) were situated in the Beqaʿ of Lebanon. Whether *ngb* (no. 57) is identical with the southernmost part of the Land of Canaan, often called Negeb in the Bible, is not clear.[25] Another identification, that of *ʾššḫn* (no. 58) with Shasḫimi, a city mentioned in an Amarna letter and situated in the Bashan, is also by no means certain.[26] The site of the other toponyms is unknown.[27]

One may conclude that the identifiable places are situated in the extreme northern and eastern parts ot Canaan, only Anaharath being a city in Galilee. It is not impossible that in this part of the list the Egyptian scribe lumped together a number of toponyms because he was not sure of their exact location, attaching the city of Anaharath to an artificial geographical group. Whatever the explanation, the topographical list of Thutmes III cannot be regarded as a key source for the location of Shemesh-edom.

25. The name *ngb* appears again in the biography of the Egyptian soldier Amenemheb (J.A. Wilson, in: *ANET*, p. 241a). It would be preferable to leave the toponym *ngb* unidentified (cf. Josh. 11:2 *ngb knrwt;* M. Goerg, "Tuthmosis III und die Shasu-Region", *JNES*, vol. 38 (1979), p. 200 n. 11).

26. W. M. Mueller, *Asien und Europa nach altaegyptischen Denkmaelern* (Leipzig 1893), p. 396; id., "Die Palaestinaliste Thutmosis III", *Mitteilungen der Vorderasiatischen Gesellschaft,* vol. 12 no. 1 (1907), p. 19; but see Borée, *Ortsnamen,* p. 57.

27. Helck (*Beziehungen,* pp. 130-131) suggested locating the entire group (nos. 49-56) in the region of Kadesh. Anaharath, however, was certainly a city in Lower Galilee.

Edel, on the other hand, argued for a northern location of Shemesh-edom on the basis of the timetable of Amenhotep's "first victorious campaign" of year seven. This campaign is described differently on two stelae. On one of them, the first date preserved is the 26th of the ninth month, and it appears directly before the crossing of the Orontes river. On the other, the first date is the 25th of the ninth month, and it appears right at the beginning of the text, even before the titles of the Pharaoh. On this stele the crossing of the Orontes river is not dated. Edel proposed combining the dates of the two stelae. Since on both stelae the capture of Shemesh-edom preceded the crossing of the Orontes he suggested that the 25th is the date for the capture of Shemesh-edom, and the 26th the date for crossing the river. Hence Shemesh-edom must have been situated one day's march from the river.

Further support for this reasoning is provided by the other campaign, that of the ninth year, described on the same two stelae.[28] There too the description starts with a date - the 25th of the third month, which is followed by the words: "His majesty proceeded to Retenu... against the town of Aphek." Does this date indicate the departure from Egypt or the conquest of Aphek? Since the description subsequently speaks of Pharaoh having reached Anaharath six days later, on what

28. Edel, "Stelen", pp. 132-146, 156-160.

happened to be the anniversary of his coronation,[29] and the distance between Anaharath and Egypt being such as could not possibly be covered in that time, the date must refer to the conquest of Aphek. One may conclude that the same method of dating is used in both descriptions of the campaigns: the first recorded date refers to the first operation of the army.

It is also significant that the Egyptian army found it necessary to cross the Orontes on its way to Qatna. If the army had been marching through Canaan from the south, its route would take it east of the Orontes, thus avoiding a crossing of the river. It must, therefore, have reached the Orontes valley not from the south but from the west. There is plenty of evidence that from the days of Thutmes III, the Egyptian army conducted campaigns by sea to the mouth of Nahr el-Kebir, advancing to inner Syria along the river (between mount Lebanon and Jebel Nusairah) up to the Orontes valley, north of Kadesh.[30] It is along this line of march, one day south of the ford of the Orontes, that one should look for the city of Shemesh-edom.

29. Edel, "Stelen", pp. 156-157; A. Alt, "Neue Berichte ueber Feldzuege von Pharaonen des Neuen Reiches nach Palaestina", *ZDPV*, vol. 70 (1954), pp. 45, 52; D.B. Redford, "The Coregency of Thutmosis III and Amenophis II", *JEA*, vol. 51 (1965), p. 121; W. J. Murnane, *Ancient Egyptian Coregencies*, Studies in Ancient Oriental Civilizations, vol. 40 (Chicago 1977), pp. 44-48.

30. A. Alt, "Das Stuetzpunktsystem der Pharaonen an der phoenikischen Kueste und im syrischen Binnenland", *ZDPV*, vol. 68 (1950), pp. 97-133 [=*KS*, vol. 3, pp. 107-140].

It may be of significance that a city named Shamshi-muruna, situated on the Phoenician coast and sending tributes to Assyria, was mentioned in the Assyrian royal inscriptions.[31] A raid conducted by the "people of the land of Iauna" against the cities of Shamshi-muruna and Ḫariṣu is mentioned in a letter from Nimrud, making it clear that both cities were located near the coast.[32] The name "Shemesh..." thus reflects a toponymic tradition known from the Lebanese coastal area in the second and first millennia B.C.

Finally, it should be pointed out that for campaigns to start from the northern boundary of Canaan was not exceptional. Indeed, all Egyptian campaigns after the battle of Megiddo and the conquest of the Land of Canaan were

31. S. Parpola, *Neo-Assyrian Toponyms,* AOAT, vol. 6 (Neukirchen-Vluyn 1970), p. 303.

32. H.W.F. Saggs, "The Nimrud Letters, 1952 - Part VI", *Iraq,* vol. 25 (1963), pp. 76-78, no. 69. The letter was sent by the Assyrian official Qurdi-Ashur-lamur, reporting to the Assyrian king that "the people of the land of Iauna have come and have made an attack on the cities of Shamshi-mu[runa], Ḫariṣu and [. . .]". It is clear therefore, that Shamshi-muruna was situated near the coast. This being so, one must reject the location of the city of Shamshi-muruna near the village of Marun, on the way leading from Tyre to the northern Huleh valley, and the association of its name with the biblical town of Shimron-meron of Josh. 12:20. See A. Alt, "Galilaeische Probleme, Teil 2: Die Assyrische Provinz Megiddo und ihr Spaeteres Schicksal", *PJb,* vol. 33 (1937), p. 66 n. 3 [=*KS,* vol. 2, p. 376 n.2]; Noth, *Josua,* p. 72.

aimed at the area under the hegemony of the kingdom of Mitanni, north of Canaan.[33] The last campaign of Thutmes III, during his 42nd year, and Amenhotep's first campaign, in his third year, were both directed to the area of Kadesh. One may conclude that the boundary between the imperial arrays of Mitanni and Egypt at the beginning of Amenhotep's reign was between Kadesh and the Land of Takhshi in the north and the Land of 'Amqi (i.e., the Beqa' of Lebanon) in the south.[34] Amenhotep's Asiatic campaigns started in this area, on the Egyptian frontier. Shemesh-edom was situated on this line, on the main route leading from the Phoenician coast to the Orontes, thus becoming the first target of Amenhotep's campaign.

As for Adamah, mentioned in the town list of the tribe of Naphtali (Josh. 19:36), it appears beside Ramah and Hazor, both situated far north of Tel Qarnei Hittin, and might perhaps be located in that area. Whether it is identical with the Adumim of the topographical list of Thutmes III (no. 36) is not clear.[35]

33. Helck, *Beziehungen*, pp. 137-160.

34. Na'aman, "Amarna", pp. 14-20; G. Kestemont, "La société internationale Mitannienne et le royaume d'Amurru à l'époque Amarnienne," *Orientalia Lovaniensia Periodica*, vol. 9 (1978), pp. 27-32.

35. Adumim appears among the toponyms of the northern Jordan valley and the eastern Jezreel plain (nos. 31-47). A location in Lower Galilee is possible, its name being equated with both the

4) The Boundary between Zebulun and Naphtali

The delineation of the eastern half of the inheritance of Zebulun (Josh. 19:12-13) was always a problem.[36] The south-eastern boundary is described in Josh. 19:12. Its line ran from Tell Shadud to Chisloth-tabor (Iksal) and Daberath (Daburiyeh), along the southern foot of the Nazareth ridge. Next comes Japhia ("then up to Japhia"), whose identification is difficult. The modern village of Yafa, which was sometimes identified with Japhia, is located west of Daburiyeh and north of the border-line, in the hill country.[37] It would be more reasonable to locate Japhia somewhere in the hilly area north of Tabor, or even on the mountain itself.

biblical village of Adami-nekeb (Josh. 19:33) and Damin of the Talmudic sources, today Khirbet et-Tell near Khirbet ed-Damiyeh. See Saarisalo, *Boundary,* pp. 31-33, 124; R. de Vaux, "Le cadre géographique du Poème de krt", *RB,* vol. 46 (1937), pp. 362-372; Klein, *Galilee, passim;* Aharoni, "Remarks", p. 180; Avi-Yonah, *Gazetteer,* p. 51. Adamah of the town list of Naphtali (Josh. 19:36) is certainly a different place and should be located further north, in the vicinity of Ramah and Hazor (cf. Abel, *Géographie,* p. 238).

36. In addition to the commentaries on the book of Joshua, note the following discussions of Zebulun's inheritance: S. Yeivin, "Zebulun", *EM,* vol. 2 (1954), pp. 896-898 [Hebrew]; Simons, *Geographical,* pp. 179-182; Aharoni, *LB,* pp. 229, 237; Kallai, *Tribes,* pp. 152-163; Taeubler, *Biblische Studien,* pp. 129-131.

37. Noth, "Studien", p. 222 n. 2; Kallai, *Tribes,* pp. 157-158.

The following verse (Josh. 19:13a) should be translated slightly differently: "From there it passes along on the east, toward the sunrise[38] – Gath-hepher (*gt hḥpr*) – to Eth-kazin". Gath-hepher is mentioned again in 2 Kings 14:25. The *h* in this case is not the article but seems to be an integral part of the name. This rendering of the verse would at once remove the difficulty created by the reference to Gath-hepher, which was universally identified with Khirbet ez-Zurra', near the village of Meshhed, 8 km. west of the assumed boundary. The border line ran along the southern and northern ends of the Nazareth hills. Gath-hepher was mentioned on account of its prominent position in the eastern part of the inheritance of Zebulun. A parallel is to be found in the appearance of Hannathon in the description of its northern boundary (Josh. 19:14).

Eth-kazin, the next border point, should perhaps be located in the neighbourhood of the village of Lubiyeh, south of the eastern end of the Beth-netophah valley.

The next part of the border is described in Josh. 19:13b-14a. This reads: "...*wyṣ' rmwnh wt'r hn'h wnsb 'tw hgbwl mṣpwn ḥntn*..."(and going on to Rimmon it bends toward Neah; then on the north the boundary turns about to

38. For this translation of the double direction *qdmh* and *mzrḥh*, compare Ex. 27:13; 38:13; Num. 2:3; 34:15. Cf. the double direction *ngb(h)* and *tymnh* in Ex. 26:18; 27:9; 36:23; 38:9; Ezek. 47:19; 48:28.

Hannathon...).[39] This gives rise to two questions: How can Rimmon fit into the border line? And what is meant by the accusative pronoun *'tw?*

Scholars have often identified Rimmon of Zebulun with the village of Rummaneh, situated on the southern side of the Beth-netophah valley. However, this location does not fit in with the expected border line. The topography of the area requires a boundary east of the Beth-netophah valley, which would continue the line described and constitute a circuit around the valley.

The only other mention of Rimmon of Zebulun in the Bible is in the list of Levitical cities (Josh. 21:35 [Dimnah = Rimmon];[40] 1 Chr. 6:77 [= MT 6:62]), which is entirely dependent upon the tribal allotments. For a comprehensive

39. Steuernagel, *Josua,* p. 226; Noth, *Josua,* p. 112. On the basis of the LXX of Josh. 19:14a many commentators omitted *'tw,* rendering the verse *wnṣb hgbwl mṣpwn ḥntn.* However, no explanation was offered for the addition, nor was the repetition of Josh. 16:6 taken into consideration (cf. Josh. 18:20). It seems to me that 'it' in these two verses is actually the key to a correct understanding of the toponyms Neah (No'ah?) and Michmethath, which were not names of towns. The identification of Michmethath and the boundary between Ephraim and Manasseh will be discussed in the next chapter [pp. 151-153].

40. For the rendering of the name Rimmon see Albright, "Levitic", pp. 64, 72.

discussion of this problem, see chapter 6 pp. 216-217. Rimmon does not appear in any post-biblical sources; only the neighbouring site of Ruma seems to have been mentioned.[41] It is for this reason that in his Onomastikon, Eusebius was unable to locate Rimmon of Zebulun. It is doubtful whether one is justified in locating the Beth-rimmon valley of Jewish sources from the Roman and Byzantine periods near the village of Rummaneh. This location is based mainly on the assumption that Rimmon was an ancient name for the site of Rummaneh.[42]

We suggest that *rmwn* of Zebulun is a metathesis of *mrwn* (Maron), copied by the compiler of the list of Levitical cities. The border of Zebulun actually reached Tel Qarnei Hittin, the most prominent site east of the Beth-netophah valley. Such a delineation would immediately clarify this and the following verse. The verb *t'r (wt'r hn'h)* was consistently

41. For Rumah, see note 18 above. The reading Damon (instead of Rimmon) was proposed by Klein (*Galilee*, pp. 57, 150 n. 16, 187), who identified the site at Khirbet ed-Damiyeh (ibid., pp. 65, 68, 152). Avi-Yonah, in his *Gazetteer,* did not mark Rimmon in the Beth-netophah valley.

42. The name Beth-netophah valley for Sahl el-Baṭṭof was known in the Talmudic sources (Avi-Yonah, *Gazetteer,* pp. 33, 40); Beth-rimmon must have indicated another valley. The identification of the valley of Beth-rimmon with the one near the village of Rummaneh seems to be a mistake, since the village is actually situated in the Beth-netophah valley.

used to describe a turn in the border-line.[43] The words following, *wnsb 'tw* (compassed it) necessarily refer to *n'h*. The logical explanation is that *n'h* (No'ah?)[44] is either a noun meaning 'valley' or a designation for the Beth-netophah valley. The border is described as surrounding (*t'r, nsb*) the valley from the northern side, leaving its most important city, Hannathon, south of the line (Josh. 19:14a).

The demarcation of the eastern boundary of Zebulun might help us to delineate the borders of the neighbouring tribe of Naphtali (Josh. 19:33-34).[45] Naphtali's southern border is not well defined, since Heleph and the oak of Zaanannim are not identified. The appearance of the two toponyms ("from Heleph, from the oak in Zaanannim" Josh. 19:33) is exceptional (but see Josh. 15:3 *mlšwn hym mqṣh hyrdn*). Heleph (*ḥlp*) is either a toponym or an unintelligible (corrupt?) word (noun?) referring to the oak of Zaanannim, which was subsequently misunderstood; and since it was

43. Baechli, "Liste", p. 8.

44. G.B. Gray, *A Critical and Exegetical Commentary on Numbers, ICC* (Edinburgh and New York 1903), p. 392.

45. In addition to the commentaries on the book of Joshua, note the following discussions of the inheritance of Naphtali: Saarisalo, *Boundary, passim;* Simons, *Geographical,* pp. 194-197; Aharoni, *Settlement,* pp. 77-86; id., *LB,* pp. 238-239; Mazar, "Sanctuary", pp. 301-302 n. 21; Kallai, *Tribes,* pp. 191-203; S. Yeivin, "Naphtali", *EM,* vol. 5 (1968), pp. 906-908 [Hebrew].

interpreted as a toponym, an extra preposition *m* (from) was attached to it (similar to *mqṣh* in Josh. 15:3 and 18:15). See the discussion of *mqṣ* (1 Kings 4:9) in chapter 2 pp. 114-115.

Next to the oak of Zaanannim comes Adami-nekeb, which was generally identified with Khirbet et-Tell near Khirbet ed-Damiyeh. In this connection, it is apposite to note Ps. 83:9-10: "Do to them as thou didst to Midian, as to Sisera and Jabin at the river Kishon, who were destroyed at En-dor, who became dung for the ground (*'dmh*)". It seems to me that the Psalmist regarded En-dor as the place where the two decisive battles – Barak against Sisera and Gideon against the Midianites – were fought.[46] Kutscher proposed that the second half of verse 10 is a pun on the place-name Adamah, located near an important ford of the Jordan (today Tell ed-Damiyeh), where Gideon and the men of Ephraim slaughtered the retreating Midianites (Judg. 7:24-25).[47] Is it possible that the second

46. The area of "Taanach, by the waters of Megiddo" (Judg. 5:19) was not the site of the battle against Sisera, but where the Canaanite army was assembled and organized for battle. See. A.F. Rainey, "The Military Camp Ground at Taanach by the Waters of Megiddo", *Eretz Israel,* vol. 15 (1981), pp. 61*-66*. En-dor (Khirbet Ṣafṣafeh) is situated at the foot of the Hill of Moreh (Jebel ed-Daḥi), on one of the tributaries of wadi Tabor, not far from the eastern tributaries of the Kishon river. It is possible that both the Canaanite troops and the Midianites camped at this site and were surprised there by the attacking Israelites.

47. Y. Kutscher, "Psalm 83:11", *BJPES,* vol. 2 (1935), pp. 40-42 [Hebrew].

half of the verse (Ps. 83:10) refers to the same two events as the first half? Adami-nekeb appears in the description of Naphtali's border next to the oak of Zaanannim, where Sisera was killed. It could be that Ps. 83:9-10 was alluding to the common features of the battles fought by Barak and Gideon: both gained their decisive victory at En-dor and won a second victory in the neighbourhood of a place called Adamah.

Next to Adami-nekeb appears Jabneel (Tell en-Na'am), and it is not clear whether the two toponyms should be located near the border, which would thus run along the valley of Jabneel, or north of it, along the modern Jabneel - Kfar Tabor road.

The continuation of the border is described thus: "then the boundary turns westward to Aznoth-tabor, and goes from there to Hukkok, touching Zebulun at the south, and Asher on the west..." (Josh. 19:34). Naphtali's southern border turned back (*šb*) to its point of departure (*ḥlp* and the oak of Zaanannim), continuing westward to Aznoth-tabor, which should be sought on the eastern border of Zebulun. One may tentatively suggest as its location Khirbet 'Irbadeh, at the eastern foot of the Nazareth hills.[48]

48. Saarisalo (*Boundary*, pp. 122-127) has identified Heleph at Khirbet 'Irbadeh and Aznoth-tabor with Umm el-Jubeil. The latter, however, is situated on an offshoot of the Nazareth hills, west of the eastern border of Zebulun. Since Khirbet 'Irbadeh is situated

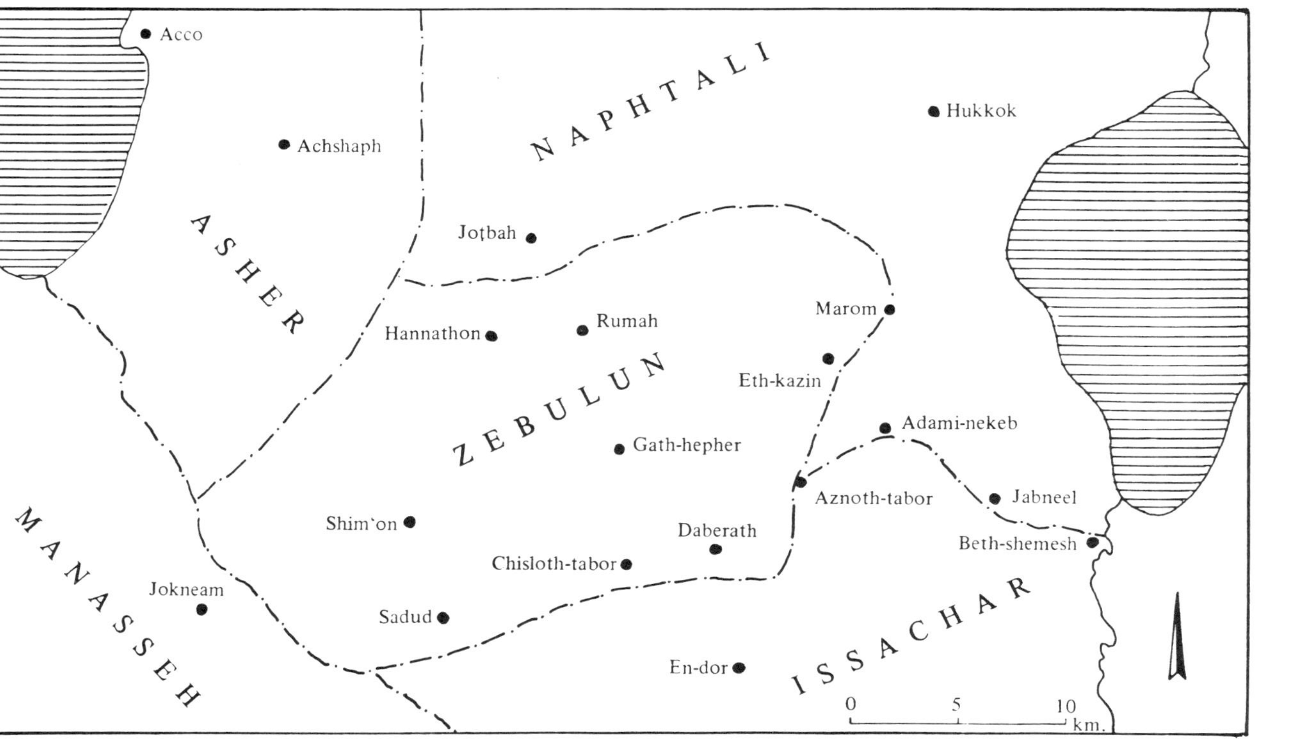

Map 4. The Inheritances of Zebulun and Naphtali.

The subsequent description of the boundary was always considered vague. However, the above identification of Maron (i.e., Rimmon) with Tel Qarnei Hittin removes the main difficulty over the delineation. Naphtali's western border ran along the eastern boundary of Zebulun from Khirbet 'Irbadeh to Tel Qarnei Hittin; its line northwards led directly to the area of Yaquq (Hukkok), which was the main settlement in this area.[49] At this point, the border turned westward along the northern boundary of Zebulun ("touching Zebulun at the south" Josh. 19:34) until it came to the western border of Asher ("and Asher on the west" Josh. 19:34). From the Yaquq area, the border might be delineated either along the northern margins of the Beth-netophah valley or along the Ṣalmon river (Wadi Rubadiyeh) and the 'Arrabeh - Sakhnin road in the direction of Cabul, which marked the eastern border of Asher (Josh. 19:27).

on the line of Zebulun's boundary, it should be identified with Aznoth-tabor, a town on the southwest corner of the inheritance of Naphtali.

49. The description of Hukkok (Yaquq) as part of the western border of Naphtali may be compared with that of Lower Beth-horon and Kiriath-jearim within the western boundary of Benjamin (Josh. 18:14). The border actually passed along the foothills on the edge of the Shephelah, but the absence of Israelite settlements along this line obliged the author of the boundary system to mark it by the nearest settlements: Lower Beth-horon on the northern side, and Kiriath-jearim on the southern side (see Kallai, *Tribes*, pp. 107-108, 112-113).

In the 14th-13th centuries B.C., Marom / Maron was a small but fortified and strategically located city-state, dependent upon the strong neighbouring kingdoms of Hazor and Shim'on. The Late Bronze Age city of Marom / Maron was located on the border of the kingdoms of Hazor and Shim'on. The site was destroyed during the 13th century B.C. and was sparsely settled by the Israelites in Iron Age I. It was again fortified in the 10th century B.C., being regarded by the author of the boundary system as a town of Zebulun bordering on the inheritance of Naphtali.

It is evident from the archaeological investigation of the site that Marom / Maron was an important fortified north Israelite city in the 9th-8th centuries B.C. Following its destruction by Tiglath-pileser III in the campaigns of years 733/732 B.C. and the deportation of its inhabitants, the city was abandoned, the ancient name possibly being transferred to the neighbouring Roman-period site of Kfar Nimrah.

CHAPTER FOUR

THE BOUNDARY BETWEEN EPHRAIM AND MANASSEH AND MOUNT EPHRAIM

1) Introduction

The border separating the tribes of Ephraim and Manasseh is described twice in the book of Joshua: first as Ephraim's northern border (Josh. 16:6-8) and the second time as Manasseh's southern border (Josh. 17:7-9). Both descriptions are far from clear and have been discussed copiously in the past fifty years.[1] In spite of the problems, a consensus about the main lines of the border has emerged.[2] The key points along this border are considered to be: the Kanah river = Wadi Qanah;

1. Research into the historical geography of the Ephraim-Manasseh boundary began in the 1930s with Elliger's article, "Grenze". The main discussions on the subject are: Noth, "Studien", pp. 201-215; Abel, "Tappouah"; K. Elliger, "Thappuah", *PJb*, vol. 33 (1937), pp. 7-22; id., "Neues"; id., "Michmethath"; Simons, "Structure"; id., *Geographical*, pp. 158-169; Jenni, "Grenze"; Wallis, "Thaanath-silo"; Kuschke, "Beitraege", pp. 102-106; Noth, "Thappuah", pp. 270-273; Kallai, *Tribes*, pp. 117-151, 374-375; L. Waechter, "Zur Lage von Michmethath", *ZDPV*, vol. 84 (1968), pp. 55-62; Otto, *Jakob*, pp. 227-245.

Tappuah = Sheikh Abu Zarad; Michmethath = Khirbet Julejil or Khirbet Kafr Beta; Taanath-shiloh = Khirbet Ta'na el-Foqa; Janoah = Khirbet Yanun.

While the western and central parts of the proposed border run along natural topographical lines, the eastern part is not so well defined. It runs right through the mountainous area south-east of Shechem. This assumed delineation is surprising, since 7-9 km. north-east of it runs the deep valley of the Tirzah river (Wadi Far'ah), which is the natural topographical boundary of the whole area. Was the tribal reality in this region so clear-cut that the author of the boundary system was obliged to mark the border in a way that conflicts with the natural topography?

Let us start our discussion of this point by examining the two texts in the book of Joshua set out below.[3]

2. An exception is the article of Eva Danelius, "The Boundary of Ephraim and Manasseh in the Western Plain", *PEQ*, vol. 89 (1957), pp. 55-67; vol. 90 (1958), pp. 32-43, 122-144, but I cannot accept the validity of her arguments.

3. In addition to the commentaries on the book of Joshua, see Simons, "Structure", pp. 206-209, 213, 215.

	Josh. 16		Josh. 17
5	The territory of the Ephraimites...	7	The territory of Manasseh reached from Asher to Michmethath, which is east of Shechem;
6	On the north is Michmethath; then on the east the boundary turns round toward Taanath-shiloh, and passes along beyond it on the east to Janoah,		
7	then it goes down from Janoah to Ataroth...		
			then the boundary goes along southward to the inhabitants of En-tappuah...
8	From Tappuah the boundary goes westward to the brook Kanah...	9	Then the boundary went down to the brook Kanah.

A comparison of the two descriptions shows that they complement each other. In the southern boundary of Manasseh, the eastern section, from Michmethath to the Jordan, is missing; and in the northern boundary of Ephraim the section from Michmethath in the north to Tappuah in the south is missing. By combining the descriptions, the entire line of the border can be reconstructed. It is clear, therefore, that whatever the explanation for the omissions, the author of the boundary system left us a complete and continuous line accurately demarcating the border between Ephraim and Manasseh.

2) The Central Section of the Border (Josh. 17:7)

The boundary dividing the inheritances of Ephraim and Manasseh is delineated by proceeding from a central point (Michmethath) and demarcating first the eastern section (Josh. 16:6-7) and then the central and western sections (Josh. 17:7-9; 16:8). The same order is used for the three Galilean tribes of Zebulun, Asher and Naphtali. After delineating one section of the southern border of those tribes, the border reverted (*šb*) to its starting point and proceeded to the other section of the border line (Josh. 19:12, 27, 34).

The description of the Ephraim-Manasseh border was split between the two tribes. Manasseh's border started at a point in the middle of the line, Michmethath, taking from there a turn southward. The author of the boundary system selected an irregular verb, *hlk* (to go), to denote the change in direction of the border.

This is not the only feature of Josh. 17:7 which has no parallel in the other descriptions of the boundary system. The use of *'l hymyn* to designate the adverbial meaning of southward is also unique; the usual word in these texts is either *ngbh* or *mngb.*[4] Furthermore, I believe that Abel was justified in rendering the meaningless *m'šr* as *m'šd* (from the

4. Abel, "Tappouah", p. 105; Baechli, "Liste", p. 9. For the use of *śm'l* to indicate the north, see Josh. 19:27 (Cooke, *Joshua,* p. 180).

slope of).[5] Again, the usual word in these descriptions for a side of a town or mountain (i.e., slope) is *ktp*.[6] The reconstructed text of Josh. 17:7 (from the slope of Michmethath which is before Shechem) may be compared with other descriptions in which *ktp* plays the same role. For example: "...the southern shoulder of the Jebusite..." (Josh. 15:8); "...along to the northern shoulder of Mount Jearim..." (Josh. 15:10); "...to the shoulder of Luz..." (Josh. 18:13); "...to the north of the shoulder of Beth-arabah..." (Josh. 18:18). The implication of this reconstruction of the text for the identification of Michmethath will be discussed below.

The exceptional features of Josh. 17:7 require an explanation. One may suggest that the author of the boundary system wanted to 'liven up' the monotonous descriptions of the border. He therefore replaced the stereotyped words with expressions that were not typical for the boundary system. This resulted in numerous textual difficulties sensed by many scholars.

5. Abel, "Tappouah", pp. 104-105; Elliger, "Neues", p. 7 n. 2; Otto, *Jakob*, p. 234 n. 3; cf. Noth, "Studien", p. 238.

6. See above p. 109 note 51. It should be pointed out that the basic meaning of *ktp* is 'side', which is common to both the border descriptions (e.g., Num. 34:11; Josh. 15:11; 18:12) as well as other biblical references (e.g., Ex. 27:14-15; 38:14-15; 1 Kings 6:8; 7:39; Ezek. 40:18, 40-41, 44; 46:19).

The original form of the text of Josh. 17:7b is usually reconstructed, with the help of LXX, as "...unto Jashi/ub to the spring of Tappuah" (in place of the meaningless "to the inhabitants of En-tappuah").[7] As a result of archaeological exploration in the vicinity of Sheikh Abu Zarad and the modern village of Yasuf, it was proposed that there was only one site in this area, called at different periods by both names - Tappuah and Jashi/ub. The words "unto Jashi/ub" were thus regarded as a very late gloss, interpolated into the original text in the Hellenistic period in order to bring it up to date, and to define more accurately the location of the spring of Tappuah.[8]

However, Jashi/ub appears in the Bible as the name of a clan of Issachar (Num. 26:24; 1 Chr. 7:1; Gen. 46:13 LXX) and in the Samaria ostraca as the name of a village in the district of (A)sriel.[9] Since the names Tappuah and Jashi/ub are found

7. Abel, "Tappouah", pp. 105-107; cf. Jenni, "Grenze", pp. 38-40; Noth, "Thappuah", pp. 270-273; Z. Kallai, "Tappuah", *EM,* vol. 8 (1982), pp. 882-883 [Hebrew]. A parallel case of the use of a spring rather than a city may be observed in Josh. 19:29. MT *'yr mbṣr ṣwr* does not make sense and many scholars agree that the text should be reconstructed, with the aid of LXX, to *'yn mbṣr ṣwr* (the spring of the Fortress of Tyre). See above p. 50.

8. Jenni, "Grenze", pp. 36-40; Noth, "Thappuah".

9. Aharoni, *LB,* pp. 223, 325 n. 101; Lemaire, "Hepher", p. 15; id., "Asriel, *šr'l,* Israel et l'origine de la confēderation Israēlite", *VT,* vol. 23 (1973), pp. 239-243.

both in the time of the Monarchy and in the Hellenistic period, they cannot refer to one and the same site. Indeed, in an archaeological survey, Iron Age pottery was discovered at Yasuf, indicating that the modern village was built on the ruins of an ancient site.[10] The detailed delineation of the border near Yasuf and the triple reference to toponyms in its vicinity can be explained by the change in the direction of the boundary at that point, and by the fact that the most important city in this area, Tappuah, remained outside Manasseh's inheritance. Jashi/ub was the nearest place to Manasseh's border, and was therefore mentioned first; then came the spring, which was on the border itself, between Jashi/ub and Tappuah; and finally, the city of Tappuah, which was situated in Ephraim's inheritance (Josh. 17:8).

Josh. 17:7 describes the central section of the Ephraim-Manasseh boundary as running south from the slope of Michmethath to Jashi/ub and the spring of Tappuah. The boundary changed direction on both sides of this line: from Michmethath it turned south-east towards the Jordan, and from the spring of Tappuah it turned west towards the Mediterranean.

3) The Eastern Section of the Border (Josh. 16:6-7)

The location of Michmethath is crucial for the correct delineation of the Ephraim-Manasseh border. From the very

10. Kallai, "Tappuah" [see note 7 above], p. 883.

beginning of modern historical geography, its identification depended on the location of the next toponym, Taanath-shiloh. The latter was commonly identified with either Khirbet Ta'na el-Foqa or Khirbet Ta'na et-Taḥta, situated 10-13 km. south-east of Shechem.[11] Michmethath was accordingly sought on the line of Shechem – Khirbet Ta'na el-Foqa and was usually located in either Khirbet Makhneh el-Foqa, Khirbet Julejil or Khirbet Kafr Beta.[12]

The article before Michmethath (*hmkmtt*) may designate a geographical object such as a mountain, hill or valley.[13] It was proposed above that Manasseh's border was drawn: from the slope (*'šd*) of Michmethath which is before Shechem (Josh. 17:7). According to this interpretation, Michmethath must have been either a mountain or a hill. It is also mentioned as the first point on Ephraim's northern border (Josh. 16:6) and just before the name something is missing in the text.[14]

11. Wallis, "Thaanath-silo", pp. 38-43, with further literature; Kallai, *Tribes*, p. 135.

12. Elliger, "Grenze", pp. 282-291; id., "Neues", pp. 7-8; id., "Michmethath"; Kuschke, "Beitraege", pp. 104-105; Waechter, op. cit., [see note 1 above]; Kallai, "Michmethath", *EM*, vol. 4 (1962), pp. 962-963 [Hebrew]; Aharoni, *LB*, p. 236; Otto, *Jakob*, pp. 234-235, 239.

13. Elliger, "Neues", p. 7 n. 2; id., "Michmethath", p. 98; Kallai, *Tribes*, pp. 128-129.

14. Steuernagel, *Josua*, p. 218; Cooke, *Joshua*, p. 155.

In the light of Josh. 17:7, as well as numerous other descriptions of the boundary system (Josh. 15:8, 10, 11; 18:12, 13, 16, 18, 19), we would suggest that the missing word was either *ktp* (side), or *'šd* (slope). The original verse would thus have run: [*mktp/m'šd*] *hmkmtt mṣpwn* - [from the side/slope] of Michmethath on the north side.

In searching for the location of Michmethath, the following two facts must be taken into consideration: (a) it was the name of a mountain or a hill situated 'before (*'l pny*) Shechem' (Josh. 17:7); (b) it was the point of departure for delineating the eastern and southern sections of the Ephraim-Manasseh border. There is only one prominence that answers these requirements, and that is Jebel el-Kabir, a relatively high mountain northeast of Shechem. Not only does this mountain stand 'before Shechem', but its northern side rises from wadi Tirzah, the deep valley forming the natural eastern end of the boundary.

Next to Michmethath in Ephraim's north-eastern border appears Taanath-shiloh (Josh. 16:6). This was always regarded as the name of a town. Alt went one step further and proposed that the second element of the name – Shiloh – distinguished it from a nearby site called Taanath-xxx, as in the case of the two neighbouring Iron Age sites of Khirbet Ta'na el-Foqa and Khirbet Ta'na et-Taḥta.[15] One may, however, propose an

15. A. Alt, "Das Institut im Jahre 1928. Teil 5: Die Reise", *PJb*, vol. 25 (1929), p. 55; Wallis, "Thaanath-silo", pp. 42-43; Z. Kallai, "Taanath-shiloh", *EM*, vol. 8 (1982), pp. 402-403 [Hebrew].

alternative explanation. It has recently been suggested that the toponym Shiloh was a *qitl* formation of *š'l* (to ask), which may mean '(place of) oracle', as indeed its temple was.[16] In the same way, Taanath-shiloh may be understood as the 'Fig tree of Oracle'. The name has exact parallels in Elon-meonenim (the Diviners' Oak - Judg. 9:37) and Elon-moreh (the oak of Moreh, i.e., oak of worship, Gen. 12:6; Deut. 11:30). It may belong to a certain group of sacred trees considered legitimate cult places in ancient Israel.[17] The appearance of Taanath-shiloh in the description of the border may be compared with the mention of the oak of Zaanannim on Naphtali's border (Josh. 19:33) both representing a well-known sacred tree near the boundary.

It is clear that both Taanath-shiloh and the village of Thena of the time of Eusebius (today Khirbet Ta'na el-Foqa) were named after the fig tree (*t'nh*). Whether both refer to the same place is open to debate. It should be emphasized that this equation of the two places, as proposed by Eusebius in his Onomastikon, still remains a very likely possibility. However, if one interprets Taanath-shiloh as the name of a sacred tree which, like the names of other sacred trees mentioned in the Bible, may have faded into oblivion when the tree perished,

16. R. Zadok, "On Five Biblical Names", *ZAW*, vol. 89 (1977), p. 267; id., "Notes on the Biblical and Extra-Biblical Onomasticon", *JQR*, vol. 71 (1980/1981), p. 109.

17. De Vaux, *Ancient Israel*, pp. 278-279; Mazar, "Sanctuary", pp. 300-303 and n. 21.

the equation with Thena is by no means certain. Only after considering the alignment of the border can one decide which solution is the more probable.

The crucial passage is Josh. 16:6-7: "...*wnsb hgbwl mzrḥh t'nt šlh w'br 'wtw mmzrḥ ynwḥh wyrd mynwḥh 'trwt...*" According to this description, the boundary turned (*nsb*) around Jebel el-Kabir eastward (*mzrḥh*). The use of the preposition in *mmzrḥ* necessarily refers to the preceding accusative pronoun (*'wtw*), and the sentence *w'br 'wtw mmzrḥ ynwḥh* should be translated: and passed it on the east towards Janoah. The end of the passage, verse 7 ("then it goes down from Janoah to Ataroth...") also indicates that Janoah was located near the boundary.[18]

The accusative pronoun *'wtw* refers to either Michmethath or Taanath-shiloh.[19] A reference to an object

18. For the name Janohah and the closely-related name Janoah, see S.E. Loewenstamm, "Janoah, Janohah", *EM*, vol. 3 (1958), pp. 704-705 [Hebrew], with further literature; Simons, *Geographical*, p. 166. For the archaeological survey of the site, see Otto, *Jakob*, pp. 212-218; id., "Survey - archaeologische Ergebnisse zur Geschichte der frueheisenzeitlichen Siedlung Janoah (Josh. 16:6-7)", *ZDPV*, vol. 94 (1978), pp. 108-118.

19. See Otto, *Jakob*, p. 210 n. 2. The omission of *'wtw* from Josh. 16:6 (Steuernagel, *Josua*, p. 217; Noth, *Josua*, p. 100) would be justified only if a proper explanation had been offered for its addition to the MT. The removal of *'wtw* was always based on the

such as a mountain (Michmethath) or a tree would be natural.[20] It is unlikely to refer to a town. But if we were to regard Taanath-shiloh as a town, *'wtw* would have to refer to the mountain of Michmethath.

We are now in a position to discuss the identity and location of Taanath-shiloh.[21] There are two possibilities.

LXX. See C.F. Burney, *The Book of Judges with Introduction and Notes* (London 1918; reprinted New York 1970), p. 318. The suggestion of Wallis ("Thaanath-silo", pp. 42-44) that *'wtw* represents the remainder of a broken name (Taanath-*'wtw*) is not convincing. [See note 20].

20. A close parallel to the use of the accusative pronoun *'wtw* in Josh. 16:6 referring to a mountain or a sacred tree, appears in the description of Zebulun's boundary (Josh. 19:13b-14a). See chapter 3 pp. 135-138. There it refers to a valley. Cf. Josh. 18:20.

21. Kallai (*Tribes*, pp. 127-138) has presented two conflicting delineations of the north-eastern border between Ephraim and Manasseh. On the one hand, he assigns the city of Shechem to Ephraim's inheritance on the basis of the list of Levitical cities, and has accepted the common identifications of Taanath-shiloh with Khirbet Ta'na el-Foqa and Janoah with Khirbet Yanun, demarcating the border along this line. On the other hand, he thinks it is possible to assign a very wide area to Taanath-shiloh and Janoah, and to mark the boundary at the edge of this territory, i.e., along wadi Tirzah. It is undoubtedly correct to regard the name of a town when used in a border delineation as referring to the outer limits of the town's land. However, in this case it is unlikely that wadi Tirzah, a deep valley, would be delineated by means of distant sites in the hills.

According to the first, Taanath-shiloh was the name of a town near but not on the boundary, and was mentioned on account of its prominence. Parallels are to be found in the descriptions of the Galilean tribes of Zebulun and Naphtali [cf. pp. 135, 138, 140]. In that case, the text of Josh. 16:6 should be read as follows: And the boundary turned eastward – Taanath-shiloh – and passed it [Michmethath] on the east towards Janoah. Taanath-shiloh would be equated with Khirbet Ta'na el-Foqa, situated not far away from the border of Ephraim. According to the second possibility, Taanath-shiloh was a sacred tree on the boundary near the banks of wadi Tirzah. The verse would then be translated: And the boundary turned eastward to Taanath-shiloh[22] and passed it [Taanath-shiloh] on the east towards Janoah.

The identification of Janoah with Khirbet Yanun, 10 km. west of wadi Tirzah, can no longer be sustained. Khirbet Yanun hardly fits even the commonly accepted line of the border, since it is located west of the Khirbet Ta'na el-Foqa - Khirbet Ta'na et-Taḥta line, while according to Josh. 16:7a, Janoah was situated on or near the border ("then it goes down from Janoah..."). Janoah should be located somewhere along wadi Tirzah, where several Iron Age II sites have been discovered.[23]

22. Compare "*wnsb hgbwl... t'nt šlh*" (the boundary turns round toward Taanath-shiloh) with Josh. 15:9 "*wt'r hgbwl b'lh*" (the boundary bends round to Baalah).

23. Z. Kallai, in: Kochavi, *Judaea,* p. 164 no. 3; R; Gophna and Y.

After Janoah the boundary reached Ataroth. Glueck's identification of Ataroth with Tell el-Mazar (known also as Tell eṣ-Ṣimadi), a site on the southern bank of wadi Tirzah and the most important mound in the north-eastern corner of Ephraim's inheritance, seems plausible and accords with our demarcation of the border.[24]

4) Mount Ephraim and the Land of Hepher

The delineation of the Ephraim-Manasseh border along wadi Tirzah may have a bearing on the long-debated problem of the confines of the first and third Solomonic districts (1 Kings 4:8, 10).[25] The first district is defined as "the hill country of Ephraim" (1 Kings 4:8) and the third as "Socoh and all the land of Hepher" (1 Kings 4:10).

Porat, in: Kochavi, *Judaea,* pp. 225-226 no. 159, p. 227 no. 174; S. Kappus, "Oberflaechenuntersuchungen im mittleren Wadi Far'a", *ZDPV,* vol. 82 (1966), pp. 81-82.

24. N. Glueck, Explorations in Eastern Palestine, IV, *AASOR,* vols. 25-28 (1951), pp. 414-419; id., "Biblical Settlements in the Jordan Valley", *Eretz Israel,* vol. 2 (1953), p. 107 [Hebrew]; Gophna and Porat, ibid., p. 229 no. 190; cf. Z. Kallai, "Ataroth", *EM,* vol. 6 (1971), pp. 165-166, with further literature [Hebrew].

25. See chapter 5. For literature on Mount Ephraim, see note 28 below. For the location of the land of Hepher, see Alt, "Israels Gaue", pp. 2-11 [=*KS*, vol. 2, pp. 77-83]; Albright, "Divisions", pp. 28-31; M. Noth, *Das System der zwoelf Staemme Israels,* BWANT, vol. IV,1 (Stuttgart 1930), pp. 125-130; W.F. Albright,

Hepher, which according to the Solomonic district system was the name of a vast territory ('land'), also appears in the genealogical lists of the Israelite tribes, among the six offspring of Manasseh (Num. 26:30-32; Josh. 17:2) and as the father of Zelophehad, who gave birth to five daughters (Num. 26:33; 27:1; Josh. 17:3). It is clear from the Samaria ostraca that what were ostensibly descendants of Manasseh were actually names of administrative districts of the Samaria hill country.[26] By identifying towns in these districts with sites in the mountains of Samaria, we are able to fix the exact location of the districts. The 'descendants' of Manasseh appearing in the Samaria ostraca are Abiezer, Helek, Asriel, Shechem, Shemida, Hoglah and Noah. Hepher is the only one of the six male descendants missing. This is not surprising when we remember that Hepher was the name of a 'land', i.e., a

"The Site of Tirzah and the Topography of Western Manasseh", *JPOS*, vol. 11 (1931), pp. 248-251; B. Maisler [=Mazar], "Die westliche Linie des Meerweges", *ZDPV*, vol. 58 (1935), pp. 78-84; R. de Vaux, "The Excavations at Tell el-Far'ah and the Site of Ancient Tirzah", *PEQ*, vol. 88 (1956), pp. 136-137; Wright, "Provinces", pp. 61*-64*; Kallai, *Tribes*, pp. 43-52; Mettinger, *Officials*, pp. 113-116; Aharoni, "Solomonic", pp. 5-10; Lemaire, "Hepher"; id., "Bene Jacob", p. 322; cf. A. Zertal, "Arubboth, Hepher and the Third Solomonic District", MA Thesis, Tel Aviv University (1980), pp. 72-104, 123-132 [Hebrew].

26. Lemaire, *Inscriptions*, pp. 21-81, with further literature; A.F. Rainey, "The Sitz im Leben of the Samaria Ostraca", *Tel Aviv*, vol. 6 (1979), pp. 91-94, with further literature.

vast area, comprising several districts of Manasseh. And indeed, both Hepher and his son Zelophehad who functions as a link between Hepher and his 'granddaughters', are omitted from the total of Manasseh's 'descendants' (Josh. 17:5). In the same way, Joseph was not enumerated in the system of the twelve tribes, since his territory was included in the allotments of Ephraim and Manasseh. In Josh. 17:5 we are told that "Thus there fell to Manasseh ten portions (*hblym*)...". These comprised five 'male' districts (Abiezer, Helek, Asriel, Shechem, Shemida) and five 'female' districts (Mahlah, Noah, Hoglah, Milcah, Tirzah). One may conclude that several of these districts were included in the land of Hepher.

Lemaire has suggested that the land of Hepher was identical with the districts of Hepher's five 'granddaughters' (i.e., the daughters of Zelophehad) and extended southwards to wadi Tirzah.[27] Since the five districts of Manasseh's 'male' descendants are known from the Samaria ostraca, their limits are easy to fix: between Tappuah (Sheikh Abu Zarad) and

27. Lemaire, "Hepher", pp. 13-20; id., *Inscriptions*, pp. 61-65, 287-289; id., "Bene Jacob", pp. 321-333; Wuest (*Untersuchungen*, pp. 64-70) suggested that the lists of Manasseh's offspring (Num. 26:30-33; Josh. 17:2-3) are not arranged geographicaly, and that the attachment of Hepher to the 'daughters' of Zelophehad is secondary and artificial. However, the arrangement of the 'male' and 'female' districts in two well-defined areas does not accord with Wuest's theory. His exclusively literary analysis does not do justice to the complexity of the problem. See H. Seebass, "Machir im Ostjordanland", *VT*, vol. 32 (1982), pp. 496-503.

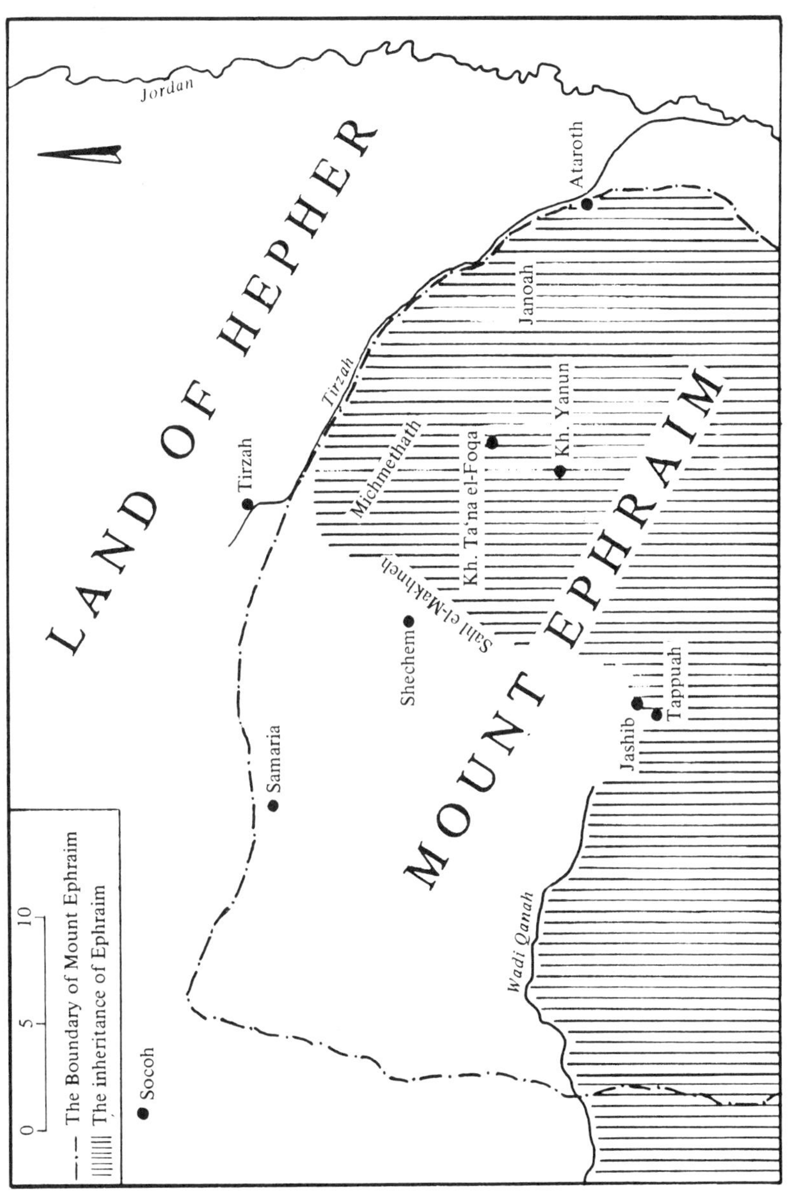

Map 5. Mount Ephraim and the Land of Hepher.

wadi Qanah in the south and the city of Samaria (Sebastiyeh) in the north. The 'male' districts thus covered the southern and western parts of the nuclear inheritance of Manasseh. The five 'female' districts (i.e., the land of Hepher) covered the northern and eastern parts of Manasseh's nuclear inheritance, between wadi Tirzah and Samaria in the south and the Jezreel valley and the Sharon in the north and west.

The southern border of Manasseh as determined in paragraphs 2 and 3 of this chapter exactly fits the confines of the 'male' and 'female' districts. Wadi Qanah was the southern border of the five 'male' districts and wadi Tirzah the southern border of the five 'female' ones. These two east-west border lines were connected by a north-south line running along what is today the main road from Jebel el-Kabir (Michmethath) through Sahl el-Makhneh to Yasuf (Jashi/ub). The north-south line demarcated the eastern confines of Manasseh's five 'male' districts adjoining the inheritance of Ephraim.

The third Solomonic district "Socoh and all the land of Hepher" (1 Kings 4:10) can now be delineated. Socoh (Khirbet Shuweiket er-Ras) was situated in the eastern Sharon, along the main road of the Land of Canaan, the so-called *Via Maris.* The district thus included the territory of the five 'female' districts (the land of Hepher) plus the eastern part of the Sharon plain.

We can now consider the northern limits of the biblical Mount Ephraim.[28] The city of Shechem is explicitly included within the confines of Mount Ephraim (Josh. 20:7; 21:21; 1 Kings 12:25; 1 Chr. 6:67 [= MT 6:52] ; cf. LXX 1 Kings 12:24o). Tola, one of the so-called 'minor Judges' and a member of the Issacharite family of Puah (Gen. 46:13; Num. 26:23; 1 Chr. 7:1), resided and was buried in Shamir in Mount

28. For the limits of Mount Ephraim in the north, see Abel, *Géographie,* p. 81 and map no. 5; S.E. Loewenstamm, "Mount Ephraim", *EM,* vol. 1 (1950), p. 513 [Hebrew] ; Noth, *History,* p. 60; id., *Josua,* pp. 125, 127; Aharoni, *LB,* pp. 26-27, 193; id., "Solomonic", pp. 5-6; Wright, "Provinces", pp. 60*-64*. Mettinger, *Officials,* pp. 113-115. The term Mount Ephraim probably means the same thing throughout the Bible. There is no justification, as far as I can see, for assuming territorial deviations at any period. *Pace* Z. Kallai, "The Biblical Geography of Flavius Josephus", *Fourth World Congress of Jewish Studies, Jerusalem 1965,* vol. 1 (Jerusalem 1967), pp. 204-205; id., *Tribes,* pp. 41-42, 390-391; id., "Baal Shalisha and Ephraim", in: *Bible and Jewish History: Studies dedicated to the memory of J. Liver,* ed. B. Uffenheimer (Tel Aviv 1972), pp. 192-195 [Hebrew] . Aharoni (*LB*, p. 193) suggested that the name was first associated only with the mountainous area where Ephraimite families settled. There is nothing to confirm this claim, since all our written sources were recorded only after the establishment of the Israelite monarchy, reflecting the territorial concepts common at that time. It seems to me that the biblical Mount Ephraim was confined to the area from the foot of Ramallah in the south to wadi Tirzah and Samaria in the north. All biblical references to Mount Ephraim tally with this definition.

Ephraim (Judg. 10:1). Shamir is most probably a variant of the name of the city Shemer/Shomron (Samaria).[29] It is known that clans of Issachar mentioned in the genealogical lists settled in the hill country, living side by side with the families of Manasseh. The fact that the families of Issachar lived near Samaria adds plausability to the suggestion that Shamir is another variant of Samaria.[30]

The inclusion of Shechem and Samaria, both parts of Manasseh's inheritance, within the limits of Mount Ephraim agrees with the description of Josh. 17:14-15. According to this passage, Joshua allotted to the sons of Joseph territories on the other side of the Jordan, because Mount Ephraim was too

29. Y. Aharoni, "Issachar and Manasseh in the Beth-shean Valley", in: *The Beth-shean Valley, the 17th Archaeological Convention of the Israel Exploration Society* (Jerusalem 1962), pp. 33, 37-38 [Hebrew]; id., *LB*, p. 223; B. Mazar, "Omri", *EM*, vol. 6 (1971), p. 304 [Hebrew]; T. Ishida, *The Royal Dynasties in Ancient Israel: A Study on the Formation and Development of Royal-Dynastic Ideology*, BZAW, vol. 142 (Berlin / New York 1977), pp. 174-175.

30. Y. Kutscher, "Where did the Tribe of Issachar Live?", *Tarbiz*, vol. 11 (1940), pp. 17-22 [Hebrew]; Herrmann, "Issakar", pp. 24-26, with further literature; Aharoni, *LB*, p. 223; Z. Kallai, "Judah and Israel: A Study in Israelite Historiography", *IEJ*, vol. 28 (1978), p. 259 n. 25; Z. Gal, "The Settlement of Issachar: Some New Observations", *Tel Aviv*, vol. 9 (1982), pp. 79-86.

small to accommodate all their families.[31] It is clear, therefore, that the tribes of both Ephraim and Manasseh – and not Ephraim alone – settled within the confines of Mount Ephraim.

The fact that families of Manasseh resided within the territory of Mount Ephraim is the clue to the northern border of the first Solomonic district (1 Kings 4:8). Its designation as a district makes it clear that it was not identical with the inheritance of Ephraim. If the writer had only the latter in mind, he would have used the name of the tribe without the appellation 'mount' (cf. 1 Kings 4:15-18).[32] Since the third district included the five 'female' districts (the land of Hepher), the first district covered Ephraim's nuclear inheritance plus the territory of the five 'male' districts (Manasseh's descendants). The northern border of these districts thus corresponds to the northern confines of Mount Ephraim. The five 'male' districts were assigned to Manasseh's inheritance within the boundary system and to the first district (Mount Ephraim) within the district system of Israel in the time of the United Monarchy.

We may conclude that wadi Tirzah, the natural topographical boundary on the east side of the mountains

31. See Noth, *Josua*, pp. 106-107; H. Seebass, "Das Haus Joseph in Jos. 17:14-18", *ZDPV*, vol. 98 (1982), pp. 70-76, with further literature on p. 70 n. 1.

32. Mettinger, *Officials*, p. 115.

of Samaria, marked both the eastern boundary between the inheritances of Ephraim and Manasseh and the eastern border between Mount Ephraim and the land of Hepher. Since both Shechem and Samaria were included within the area of Mount Ephraim, its northern border with the land of Hepher probably ran parallel to the modern Samaria - Tul Karem road. The northern border of the five 'male' districts of Manasseh also ran along this line. Both Tirzah and Samaria, the two future capitals of the Northern Kingdom, were located on the same border, between Mount Ephraim and the land of Hepher. The three main Canaanite cities of Tappuah, Shechem and Tirzah, all of which became important Israelite centres, were situated along the boundary between the inheritances of Ephraim and Manasseh. It is clear that both the natural topography of the hill country and the disposition of the Canaanite city-states had an important influence on the pattern of settlement of the Israelites in this mountainous area. The biblical records reflect exactly the geographical and historical situation in this region during the time of the Monarchy.

CHAPTER FIVE

THE DISTRICT SYSTEM IN THE TIME OF THE UNITED MONARCHY (1 KINGS 4:7-19)

The record of the high officials serving under Solomon in 1 Kings 4 includes a list of the governors appointed for the various districts. Since the officials were the most important element of that document, the districts were only described in an abridged form, to provide a general picture of their location. Occasionally, because of the difficulty of abridging a description, a more elaborate one was given.

The short descriptions have been a stumbling-block ever since the early days of historical geography, and many scholars have attempted to interpret the list.[1] Numerous

1. These are the main studies dealing with the problem of the Solomonic districts: Alt, "Israels Gaue"; Albright, "Divisions", pp. 25-36; Abel, *Géographie,* pp. 79-83 and map 5; Wright, "Provinces"; Kallai, *Tribes,* pp. 35-62; Pintore, "Intendenti"; Mettinger, *Officials,* pp. 111-127; Aharoni, "Solomonic"; M. Noth, *Koenige, BK,* vol. 9 (Neukirchen-Vluyn 1968), pp. 55-58, 66-75; D.B. Redford, "The Taxation System of Solomon", in: *Studies on the Ancient Palestinian World, presented to F.V. Winnett,* eds. J.W. Wevers and D.B. Redford (Toronto 1972), pp. 141-156; J. Bright, "The Organization and Administration of the Israelite Empire", in: *Magnalia Dei, The Mighty Acts of God, Essays on the Bible and Archaeology in Memory of G.E. Wright,* eds. F.M. Cross,

problems have been solved; some questions have either remained unanswered or are still disputed. As a result of progress in the study of the historical geography of the country and because of our better understanding of the administrative structure of the kingdoms of the ancient Near East, it is now possible to clarify some of the remaining problems of the Solomonic district system.

To facilitate the discussion, we shall first designate the districts consecutively:[2]

District I	-	Mount Ephraim
Distirct II	-	The inheritance of Dan (enlarged)
District III	-	Socoh and all the land of Hepher
Distirct IV	-	The region of Dor
District V	-	The Jezreel and Beth-shean plains
District VI	-	The towns of Jair in Gilead and the region of Argob in Bashan
District VII	-	Mahanaim
Distirct VIII	-	Naphtali
Distirct IX	-	Asher and Zebulun
Distirct X	-	Issachar
District XI	-	Benjamin
District XII	-	The land of Judah

W.E. Lemke and P.D. Miller (Garden City, New York 1976), pp. 197-201. For a more detailed list, see Aharoni, ibid., pp. 14-15.

2. There are several discrepancies between the list below and MT. These will be discussed in what follows.

1) Background and Date

Mettinger pointed out that although the district system in general followed the tribal boundaries, in some cases it did not do so, and he thinks the reason was political: that Solomon tried to weaken the House of Jospeh by encroaching upon its area.[3]

This idea of cutting up the territory of the House of Joseph into several districts presupposes that the House of Joseph actually possessed an extensive territory. But when we examine the relevant passages – Josh. 16; 17:7-13; Judg. 1:27-29 – we discover that the tribal allotments include, in addition to the nuclear tribal areas, new areas which had never been part of the tribal inheritance, and which were only theoretically attached to the tribes. In other words, the inclusion of the 'Canaanite' districts in the inheritances of Ephraim and Manasseh is the result of a literary process. The author of the boundary system devised an extensive territory for Joseph to suit the logic of his composition [see chapter 2 pp. 88-95]. It has no basis in actual fact. On the other hand, in 1 Kings 4 the division of these areas into 'Canaanite' districts (II, IV and V) and the nuclear tribal districts of Ephraim and Manasseh (I and III), reflects the reality of the two tribes within the United Monarchy.

We may therefore conclude that the division into districts was not directed against the House of Joseph and that the

3. Mettinger, *Officials*, pp. 119-120; cf. Albright, *Religion*, p. 140.

separation of the newly-conquered 'Canaanite' entities from the districts of the House of Joseph had no connection with the actual power and influence of Ephraim and Manasseh in the Israelite kingdom.

Wright suggests that the arrangement of the districts was a radical change from the tribal system, and that in forming the new districts an effort was made to standardize their economic capacity.[4] But a close examination does not support his theory. Districts IV (Dor), IX (Issachar) and XI (Benjamin) do not bear economic comparison with the larger and richer districts.

For further clarification of the problem of the historical growth of districts and the demands imposed on the newly organized units, we should look at the administrative division of the kingdom of Assyria. The land of Assyria was divided into districts of roughly the same size, each headed by a governor. When Assyria started expanding in the 9th century B.C., its rulers annexed the territories of neighbouring kingdoms. They were inclined to base their administrative arrangements in the annexed kingdoms on the local systems they found already in operation. On several occasions, an annexed kingdom was regarded as a single administrative

4. Wright, "Provinces", p. 59*. Wright's claims were refuted by Mettinger (*Officials*, pp. 116-117) and Aharoni ("Solomonic", pp. 12-13).

district.[5] The result of these annexations was a distinct difference in size between the old and the new Assyrian provinces. The burden of taxes and levies imposed on the inhabitants of newly-conquered provinces was certainly not lighter than on long-established inhabitants of the kingdom. Therefore the demands on districts of different size and population could not have been equal.

This example may serve as a general model for the ancient Near East, and one can safely assume that a somewhat similar process was taking place in Israel. When, in the course of his conquests, David annexed vast areas to the Israelite kingdom, the division into districts was made according to local conditions, resulting in territorial inequalities and differences in economic capacity. As far as the individual was concerned, however, the levies and taxes remained roughly the same throughout the newly-established kingdom.

5. Forrer, *Provinz*, pp. 5-11; P. Garelli and V. Nikiprowetzky, *Le Proche-Orient Asiatique. Les Empires Mésopotamiens Israel*, Nouvelle Clio (Paris 1974), pp. 229-233; Garelli, "Les sujets du rois d'Assyrie", in: *La voix de l'opposition en Mésopotamie: Colloque organisé par l'Institut des Hautes Etudes de Belgique* (1973), pp. 189-192; P. Machinist, "Provincial Governance in Middle Assyria and Some New Texts from Yale", *Assur*, vol. 3 no. 2 (1982), pp. 12-34.

It was realised long ago that in MT Judah is absent from the district system. Alt, in 1913, thought the districts included only Northern Israel in the limited meaning of that term. This is a direct outcome of his overall view that Judah and Israel, during the entire monarchial period, were two distinct entities, joined for only a brief period during the United Monarchy as result of a personal union (*Personalunion*).[6] Others have not only regarded the MT as the original text, but have also used it as a key to their interpretation of the purpose of the entire district system.

In 1950 Mazar suggested that the system originated in the United Monarchy and was intended for the levy of taxes in kind "...except for Judah, which was exempted from the tax...".[7]

Two points must, however, be emphasized:

(a) In the ancient Near East as well as ancient Israel, districts were used for various purposes, including the conscription of military and labour forces, the collection of taxes in kind and other payments, and perhaps even the supply of temple offerings and sacrifices.[8]

(b) Exemptions were rare, and were granted only to certain important individuals, such as influential state employees,

6. Alt, "Israels Gaue", pp. 18-19 [=*KS*, vol. 2, pp. 88-89]; id., "Staatenbildung", pp. 52-78 [=*KS*, vol. 2, pp. 42-65].

7. B. Mazar, "Eretz Israel", *EM*, vol. 1 (1950), p. 711 [Hebrew].

8. The kingdom of Assyria in the 9th-7th centuries B.C. is a good

in recognition of faithful service to the monarch. The rule was that taxes and levies were imposed on all sections of the population, the main exception being the inhabitants of the Babylonian shrine cities, who gained their *immunitas* by a long and complicated process.[9]

It therefore seems to me that in no circumstances could the people of Judah have been exempted from all the taxes and levies imposed by Solomon.

example of the division into districts and the levies and taxes imposed on them by the central government. See Forrer, *Provinz, passim;* J.N. Postgate, *Taxation and Conscription in the Assyrian Empire,* Studia Pohl, Series Maior vol. 3 (Rome 1974), *passim.* It should be emphasized that a single territorial division for all the administrative functions of the central government is common to all kingdoms of the Fertile Crescent in the 2nd and 1st millennia B.C., and is not exclusive to the kingdom of Assyria.

9. For exemptions in Mesopotamia, see F.R. Kraus, "Ein mittelbabylonischer Rechtsterminus", in: *Symbolae Iuridicae et Historicae Martino David Dedicatae,* eds. J.A. Ankum, R. Feenstra and W.F. Leemans, vol. 1 (Leiden 1968), pp. 9-40; "Kidinnu, Kidinnutu", *The Chicago Assyrian Dictionary,* vol. K (1971), pp. 342b-345a, with further literature; H. Reviv, "Kidinnu (Observations on Privileges of Mesopotamiam Cities)", *Shnaton,* vol. 2 (1977), pp. 205-216 [Hebrew] ; Postgate, ibid., pp. 238-244; cf. H. Tadmor, "Shrine City and Royal City in Babylonia and Assyria", in: *Holy War and Martyrology: Town and Community.* Lectures delivered at the eleventh and twelfth conventions of the Historical Society of Israel (Jerusalem 1967), pp. 179-205 [Hebrew] .

Aharoni wondered whether the Solomonic division into districts was intended "to punish or reward different tribes by imposing on them an equal yearly taxation in spite of their different potentials". It is impossible to guess how he would answer this question.[10] Aharoni also claimed that Judah was not included in the district system, having a privileged status in the kingdom: "...the antipathy between Judah and Israel was officially recognized in the administration of the kingdom".

The place of the land of Judah within the district system now requires more detailed examination. According to the MT, Judah was not included in the system, the twelve districts comprising the inheritances of only the ten northern tribes. However, in view of the preceding discussion, the absence of Judah is strange. Indeed, some scholars have proposed that the word 'Judah' was dropped at the end of 1 Kings 4:19 due to haplography. This is supported by the text of the LXX^{B}.[11] According to this emendation of MT, the twelfth district is represented as "And there was one officer in the land of Judah", without mentioning the name of the governor.

10. Aharoni, "Solomonic", pp. 13-14, writes: "This seems very probable". In the revised edition of his book (*LB*, p. 316) he answers the same question: "This seems very improbable".

11. See inter alii: Montgomery, *Kings,* pp. 121-123, 126; M. Noth, *Koenige, BK* vol. 9 (Neukirchen-Vluyn 1964), p. 58; Kallai, *Tribes,* pp. 38-40, with further literature; Mettinger, *Officials* pp. 121-124.

A decisive argument in favour of this proposition is provided by an analysis of the structure of the district system. The districts in the centre of the country, encompassing the tribal inheritances of Dan, Ephraim and Manasseh (Districts I-V), are mentioned first. They are followed by the Transjordanian areas (Districts VI-VII), the second half of Manasseh being the link connecting them to the former group. Then come the northern tribes (Districts VIII-X), and finally the southern tribes (Districts XI-XII). Verse 19 "Geber, the son of Uri, in the land of Gilead...", adding another Transjordanian district, is obviously out of place, and does not fit this consecutive arrangement of the districts. The expression 'all Israel' is used twice in this chapter (1 Kings 4:1, 7), indicating that the redactor had the entire kingdom of Israel in mind. It would seem, therefore, that in spite of the absence of the name of the governor in this instance, the original text was *b'rs yhwdh* ("in the land of Judah") and that Judah was part of the district system.

Another indication of a textual interference in verse 19 is to be found in the spelling of נציב . Solomon's prefects are repeatedly called נצבים in the descriptions of his reign (1 Kings 4:5, 7, 27 [= MT 5:7] ; 5:16 [= MT 5:30] ; 9:23; cf. also 2 Chr. Q 8:10). On the other hand נציבים was the title of governors of foreign countries, either Philistines in the land of Israel (1 Sam. 10:5; 13:3, 4; cf. 1 Chr. 11:16) or Israelites in Aram (2 Sam 8:6) and Edom (2 Sam. 8:14). Only in the late tradition of the book of Chronicles are the Israelite prefects called נציבים (2 Chr. K 8:10; 17:2). It is thus clear that the appearance of the title נציב in 1 Kings 4:19 came from the hand of a late writer, working at a time when the difference between נציב and נצב had been forgotten.

As has been suggested by several commentators, most of verse 19, where a third Transjordanian district seemingly appears, must be regarded as an interpolation.

It seems to me that the additional verse was inserted by a Judaean writer in order to conceal the fact that the tribe of Judah had at one time been included by Solomon in his heavy taxation system.[12] In his effort to disguise an unpleasant fact, the late Judaean writer, when revising the text, created a third Transjordanian district by combining a variation of District VI (v. 13) with a quotation from the description of the conquest of Transjordan by the Israelite tribes. By the addition of this artificial twelfth district, the land of Judah ostensibly remained outside the district system. Luckily, as so often happens, fragments of the original text escaped this editorial activity, and it is therefore still possible to reconstruct it.[13]

There is no doubt that the list of governors and their districts originated in the reign of Solomon, but the exact date

12. This is similar to what the Chronicler (2 Chr. 2:17 [= MT 2:16]) did to 'improve' the text of 1 Kings 5:13 [= MT 5:27] with regard to the forced labour imposed by Solomon on the people of Israel.

13. For other instances of the bias of Judaean scribes, see chapter 1 pp. 64-66.

is unknown. Of two governors (the sons of Abinadab and Ahimaaz, vv. 11 and 15), it is related that they were Solomon's sons-in-law, and this information may help us to narrow down the possible period during which the governors served. Solomon was co-regent with David and was apparently crowned three years before his father's death.[14] Solomon's son Rehoboam was 41 years old when he ascended the throne (1 Kings 14:21), and since Solomon reigned for 40 years (1 Kings 11:42), Rehoboam must have been born in David's lifetime. This being so, and remembering that girls married very young in the ancient Near East, it is feasible that Solomon had daughters of marriageable age by the second decade of his reign. Thus the list of governors, including Solomon's sons-in-law, can be dated to some time from the second decade of his reign onward.[15]

14. S. Yeivin, "David", *EM*, vol. 2 (1954), p. 637 [Hebrew]; T. Ishida, *The Royal Dynasties in Ancient Israel: A Study on the Formation and Development of Royal Dynastic Ideology*, BZAW, vol. 142 (Berlin/New York 1977), pp. 153-154, 170; cf. E. Ball, "The Co-Regency of David and Solomon (1 Kings 1)", *VT*, vol. 27 (1977), pp. 268-279.

15. For the discussions of the governors' dates, see Y. Aharoni, "The Districts of Israel and Judah", in: *The Kingdoms of Israel and Judah*, ed. A. Malamat (Jerusalem 1961), pp. 112-114 [Hebrew]; Kallai, *Tribes*, pp. 35-36; Mettinger, *Officials*, p. 112; B. Halpern, "Sectionalism and the Schism", *JBL*, vol. 93 (1974), pp. 529-530. Mettinger suggested that Ahimaaz, the governor of the eighth district, might be identical with the son of Zadok, David's high priest (2 Sam 15:27); that Baana, son of Hushai, the governor of the ninth district, was in all probability the son of 'David's friend'

More important than dating the list of governors is dating the establishment of the district system. In order to fix a date for a district system, one needs first to establish the historical setting of the districts. Alas, our writer did not supply the data that would enable us to determine the external boundaries of the complete system. It is known that the plain of Acco (1 Kings 9:11-13) and probably also extensive territories in Transjordan (1 Kings 11:23-25) were lost to Israel in the latter half of Solomon's reign.[16] But whether these losses are reflected in the district system cannot be determined, because of the abridged, schematic manner in which the districts were described. Let us take as an example, District IX. This is said to be "in Asher and *b'lwt*" (1 Kings 4:16), from which it is impossible to determine whether the plain of Acco is included or not [but cf. pp. 192-193]. Assertions that the list of districts reflects the reduction in the size of the kingdom in the second half of Solomon's reign are based entirely on supposition and certainly not on the descriptions of the

(2 Sam 15:37); and that Baana, son of Ahilud, the governor of the fifth district, was probably the brother of David's and Solomon's 'recorder' (2 Sam 8:16; 20:24; 1 Kings 4:3). Halpern also proposed identifying Abinadab, son of Iddo, as the son of Iddo who ruled Manasseh in Gilead in the time of David (1 Chr. 27:21). All these additional data, however, do not yield a more accurate date for the list of the governors.

16. Aharoni, *LB*, pp. 275-277.

districts.[17] The absence of information about the precise external boundaries of the district system obliges us to look for other methods of dating its establishment.

The kingdom of Solomon was a direct continuation of the great kingdom founded by his father. Furthermore, territorial divisions are long-enduring, since they are basically dependent on the physical conformation of the land, tending to change only as a result of a severe political crisis or total change

17. The discussion about the extent of the ninth district may serve as an example of a debate influenced by a priori arguments. Scholars have been inclined to assume that the plain of Acco was not included within the district system. See: Albright, "Divisions", p. 29; Abel, *Géographie,* p. 82 and map 5; Wright, "Provinces", p. 60*; Pintore, "Intendenti", p. 179; Aharoni, "Solomonic", pp. 8-9. Aharoni (op. cit. [note 15 above], pp. 112-113), in order to strengthen his assumption, claimed that the towns of the plain of Acco should have appeared as a separate 'Canaanite' district, and not as part of an Israelite tribal inheritance. However, this claim is based on an a priori argument that the districts of city-state origin were systematically separated from those of tribal origin. As will be demonstrated below, the distinction between the two kinds of districts was not followed consistently and some were of a mixed nature. Furthermore, the phrase "in Asher and *b'lwt*" (1 Kings 4:16), refers to the enlargement of the territory of the inheritance of Asher. The obscure name *b'lwt* seems to increase, and certainly does not reduce, the size of the allotment (see Kallai, *Tribes,* p. 57).

of regime.[18] One might therefore assume that the district system had been established by David after he completed his conquests.[19] In what follows, an attempt will be made to show that this division reflects even older circumstances.

One must now examine the descriptions of 1 Kings 4:7-19, especially those difficult verses whose interpretation is still disputed.

2) Text and Historical Geography.

The First and Third Districts

The first district is defined as "Mount Ephraim". Its western confines are different from those of the inheritance of Ephraim, which in the west reached the Mediterranean, thus including

18. Alt, "Landnahme", pp. 2-4 [=*KS*, vol. 1, pp. 90-92]; cf. Alt, "Provinzen", pp. 228-237 [=*KS*, vol. 2, pp. 194-201]; K. Elliger, "Die Nordgrenze des Reiches Davids", *PJb*, vol. 32 (1936), pp. 45-59.

19. This assumption was examined briefly by Alt ("Staatenbildung", pp. 62-63 [=*KS*, vol. 2, pp. 51-52]; "Stadtstaat", p. 15 [=*KS*, vol. 3, pp. 265-266]), and was accepted by Mazar ("Dan", p. 71) and by Yeivin ("The Administration in Ancient Israel (Under David)", in: *The Kingdoms of Israel and Judah* [see note 15 above], pp. 51-53). It is diametrically opposed to the opinions of Aharoni (*LB*, pp. 267, 277) and Gottwald (*Tribes*, pp. 362-375), who proposed that the administration established by David was replaced by Solomon.

the Sharon coast and the area around Gezer (Josh. 16:3, 5-6, 8). Mount Ephraim did not include these. The Sharon coast was included in District IV and Gezer in District II. The southern limits of Mount Ephraim and the inheritance of Ephraim were identical.[20]

The northern border of Mount Ephraim is disputed. Some have assumed that Mount Ephraim extended over the entire nuclear inheritances of Ephraim and Manasseh.[21] Kallai, however, proposed that Mount Ephraim corresponded to Ephraim's allotment, i.e., that its northern border was identical

20. It would seem that the name of Benjamin ('son of the south') was given to the southern tribe of the House of Joseph on account of his position south of Mount Ephraim, the seat of the tribe of Ephraim and part of the tribe of Manasseh. A different opinion was expressed by Z. Kallai ("Baal Shalisha and Ephraim", in: *Bible and Jewish History, Studies Dedicated to the Memory of J. Liver,* ed. B. Uffenheimer (Tel Aviv 1971), pp. 191-195 [Hebrew]), suggesting that Mount Ephraim sometimes covered areas of the inheritance of Benjamin. Arguments that Mount Ephraim's southern border always corresponded with the border separating the inheritances of Ephraim and Benjamin will be advanced elsewhere.

21. Abel, *Géographie,* p. 81; S.E. Loewenstamm, "Mount Ephraim" *EM,* vol. 1 (1950), p. 513 [Hebrew]; Noth, *Josua,* pp. 125, 127; id., *History,* p. 60; Aharoni, *LB,* pp. 26-27, 193; id., "Solomonic", pp. 8-9; Pintore, "Intendenti", pp. 179, 198.

to the boundary of the inheritance of Ephraim.[22] The resolution of this controversy depends on the district system, or, to be more exact, on the correct demarcation of the confines of Mount Ephraim's northern neighbour, the third district.

The third district is described thus: "Ben-hesed, in Arubboth (to him belonged Socoh and all the land of Hepher)" 1 Kings 4:10. Zertal suggested locating Arubboth, the centre of the district, in the hilly area in the south of the valley of Dothan, at Khirbet el-Ḥammam. Socoh was certainly located in the eastern plain of Sharon (Khirbet Shuweiket er-Ras), on the main road from the Shephelah to the plain of Jezreel. The city of Hepher (Josh. 12:17), which was in the land of Hepher, was identified by Zertal with Tell el-Muḥafar, on the northern side of the plain of Dothan.[23]

The key to the delineation of the third district is the term "the land of Hepher". In chapter 4 [pp.158-162] we came to the conclusion that this encompassed the territory of the five

22. Kallai, *Tribes,* pp. 41-42, 127, 390-391.

23. A. Zertal, "Arubboth, Hepher and the Third Solomonic District", MA Thesis, Tel Aviv University (Tel Aviv 1980), pp. 123-137 [Hebrew]. It should be emphasized that Wright ("Provinces", pp. 62*-63*) had already argued for a location of Hepher in the area north of Shechem. Cf. V. Fritz, "Die sogenannte Liste der besiegten Koenige in Josua 12", *ZDPV,* vol. 85 (1969), p. 149; Mettinger, *Officials,* p. 114.

'daughters' of Zelophehad, extending between wadi Tirzah and the city of Samaria to the south, the plain of Jezreel to the north, and the plain of Sharon to the west.

From this we can deduce that the southern limit of the third district is identical to the southern limit of the land of Hepher, which is the northern border of Mount Ephraim or the first district. Thus, Mount Ephraim must have comprised the mountainous sections of Ephraim's inheritance, plus the area of the five 'sons' of Manasseh [see pp. 158-166].

The question now remains, to which district did the eastern Sharon belong? It was probably divided between Districts I and III. District III, as we have just shown, included the mountainous areas called the land of Hepher, as well as a strip of the Sharon indicated by Socoh.[24] In the later system of the Assyrian provinces, the city of Aphek was associated with the district of Samaria and not with its western neighbour, the province of Dor. Recalling how conservative administrative divisions are, we may assume that the eastern parts of the Sharon plain, between Socoh and Aphek, were part of District I.

24. The same geographical conclusions were reached by Albright ("Divisions", p. 29), Wright ("Provinces", pp. 62-64) and Mettinger (*Officials*, pp. 113-116).

The Second District

This is defined as: The son of Deker, from the end of Shaalbim and Beth-shemesh and Aijalon to Beth-hanan,[25] an area almost identical to the inheritance of Dan. The problems relating to this inheritance were discussed in chapter 2 [pp.107-116]. It was proposed there that the second district was defined by four border points: Shaalbim in the north; Beth-shemesh in the south; Aijalon in the east; Beth-hanan in the west. If this translation and interpretation of the verse is correct, and the second district is defined by these four points, a glance at the map makes it plausible that Gezer and the neighbouring areas were part of the second district, whereas in the boundary system Gezer was included in the inheritance of Ephraim (Josh. 16:3). As far as we can see, this is the only difference between the second district and the inheritance of Dan.

The Fourth District

"Ben-abinadab, in all Naphath-dor (he had Taphath the daughter of Solomon as his wife)" 1 Kings 4:11 describes the fourth district. The term *nph* must have designated a certain characteristic of the district of Dor; its exact meaning, however, is disputed.[26] The size of this district is unknown, and can be

25. For a justification of this translation, see above pp. 114-115.

26. M. Ben-Dov, "*nph* - A Geographical Term of Possible 'Sea-People' Origin", *Tel Aviv*, vol. 3 (1976), pp. 70-73, with further literature. The main conclusions of this article: the word *nph* originated from

determined only from the delineation of its three neighbours. As was suggested above, the eastern parts of the Sharon plain were included in the first and third districts. The second district extended up to the line of wadi Aijalon and the Jarkon river, matching the western boundary of the inheritance of Dan (Josh. 19:46). Consequently, "all *npt* Dor" meant the narrow strip of the Sharon coast, between mount Carmel in the north and the Jarkon river in the south. Thus District IV bordered on the land of the Philistines in the south and the plain of Acco, beyond the Carmel, in the north.[27]

one of the Sea Peoples' languages and means 'a forest in the plain', parallel to the word Sharon in Semitic; and both *nph* and Sharon designated the forested area along the coastal plain. However, in the list of Canaanite kings in Josh. 12, "the king of Aphek of the Sharon" (according to the LXX) and "the king of Dor *lnpt* Dor" appear side by side, indicating that Sharon and *npt* Dor, were not exactly parallel terms for the same district. Further, the word Sharon appears only in the singular, while *nph* appears both in the singular and in the plural (cf. Josh. 11:2). Also, 'a forest in the plain' does not fit the description of Josh. 11:2. Finally, the number of words the Hebrew language absorbed from the Sea Peoples' languages is so small that one would hesitate to look for a solution in this direction. The denomination *nph* related exclusively to Dor and certainly describes a particular characteristic of this area. Its exact meaning, however, still evades us.

27. This delineation of the fourth district was first suggested by Albright ("Divisions", pp. 29, 31-32) and was accepted by Ben-Dov [see note 26 above].

The shape and size of District IV make one wonder why anyone should choose to designate this awkward area as a district. The answer lies in its geographical pecularities, its ethnic and historical past, and its economy. In the 12th-11th centuries B.C., one of the groups of the 'Sea Peoples', the Siceloi, had settled on this narrow stretch of coast. Since it consisted largely of inaccessible sand dunes, swamps and forests, the population had to concentrate mainly in and around the capital, Dor, and in small hamlets along the coast (e.g., Tel Shiqmona, Tel Mevorakh, Tel Mikhal, Tell Kudadi, Tell Qasileh). Economically, this meant small-scale agriculture, fishing and perhaps also maritime trade. It was these factors that helped the inhabitants of the Sharon coast to retain their independence until David's conquests. Because of the pecularities of the area, it was organized as a separate unit within the district system.

These pecularities also influenced the Assyrians, after conquering and annexing parts of the land in 733/732 B.C., to create a separate province along the sea-shore, which they called by the name of its capital city, Dor. It is mentioned both in an Assyrian administrative list, which recorded only the names of provinces, and in a geographical list, where the Assyrian provinces were enumerated together with the neighbouring kingdoms of the Assyrian Empire.[28] The Assyrian province seems to have replaced the Israelite district of Dor established by David, and it apparently remained unchanged during the monarchial period.

The Fifth District

The verse describing the fifth district, "Baana the son of Ahilud, in Taanach, Megiddo, and all Beth-shean which is beside Zarethan below Jezreel, and from Beth-shean to Abel-meholah, as far as the other side of Jokmeam" (1 Kings 4:12), is certainly corrupt. I believe that Albright was right in rendering it as follows: "Baana, son of Ahilud, Taanach and Megiddo as far as beyond Jokneam, and all Beth-shean below Jezreel, from Beth-shean to Abel-meholah which is near Zarethan".[29] The district was defined by describing its two main geographical regions: the plains of Jezreel and Beth-shean. The plain of Jezreel covered the area between the former city-states of Taanach, Meggido and Jokneam, the latter being a marginal town in the inheritance of Manasseh, near the western border

28. Forrer, *Provinz,* pp. 52, 54, 59-60, 69; Alt, "Provinzen", pp. 234-237 [=*KS,* vol. 2, pp. 199-201]. All the documents published after the appearance of Forrer's book support his basic claim about the nature of the sources on which he founded his conclusions. Surprisingly, however, it has recently been claimed, without any supporting argument, that Dor was not an independent province, but only part of the district of Samaria. See I. Eph'al, "Assyrian Domination in Palestine", in: *The Age of the Monarchies: Political History,* ed. A. Malamat, in: *The World History of the Jewish People,* First Series: Ancient Times, vol. 4 (Jerusalem 1979), pp. 285-286; A.F. Rainey, "Toponymic Problems: The Way of the Sea", *Tel Aviv,* vol. 8 (1981), pp. 146-147.

29. Albright, "Divisions", p. 26.

of Zebulun (Josh. 19:11).[30] That Albright's change of spelling (*yqn'm* instead of *yqm'm*) is correct, is evident not only from the geographical context, but also from the fact that there was another place called Jokmeam in Ephraim's inheritance (1 Chr. 6:68 [= MT 6:53]), far away from the southern border of the Solomonic fifth district.

The plain of Beth-shean lay between the cities of Beth-shean and Abel-meholah, which was identified with Tell Abu Ṣuṣ, near the Jordan on the natural geographical boundary of the plain of Beth-shean.[31] Zarethan (Tell es-Sa'idiyeh[?]) was situated on the other side of the Jordan, and in Solomon's time was better known than Abel-meholah, because of its importance in the copper industry and the casting of bronze vessels (1 Kings 7:46). That was why the writer included Zarethan as an additional indication of the district's southern border.

30. The old name of this plain was "Gina", mentioned both in the annals of Thutmes III and in one of the Amarna letters. N. Na'aman, "Royal Estates in the Jezreel Valley in the Late Bronze Age and Under the Israelite Monarchy", *Eretz Israel,* vol. 15 (1981), p. 143 [Hebrew].

31. Zobel, "Abel-mehola"; N. Zori, "Abel-Meholah", *BIES,* vol. 31 (1967), pp. 132-135 [Hebrew]. Tell Abu Ṣuṣ is situated near the point where the eastern slopes of the hills come close to the Jordan valley, in the area which is the natural southern border of the plain of Beth-shean and the beginning of the central Jordan valley.

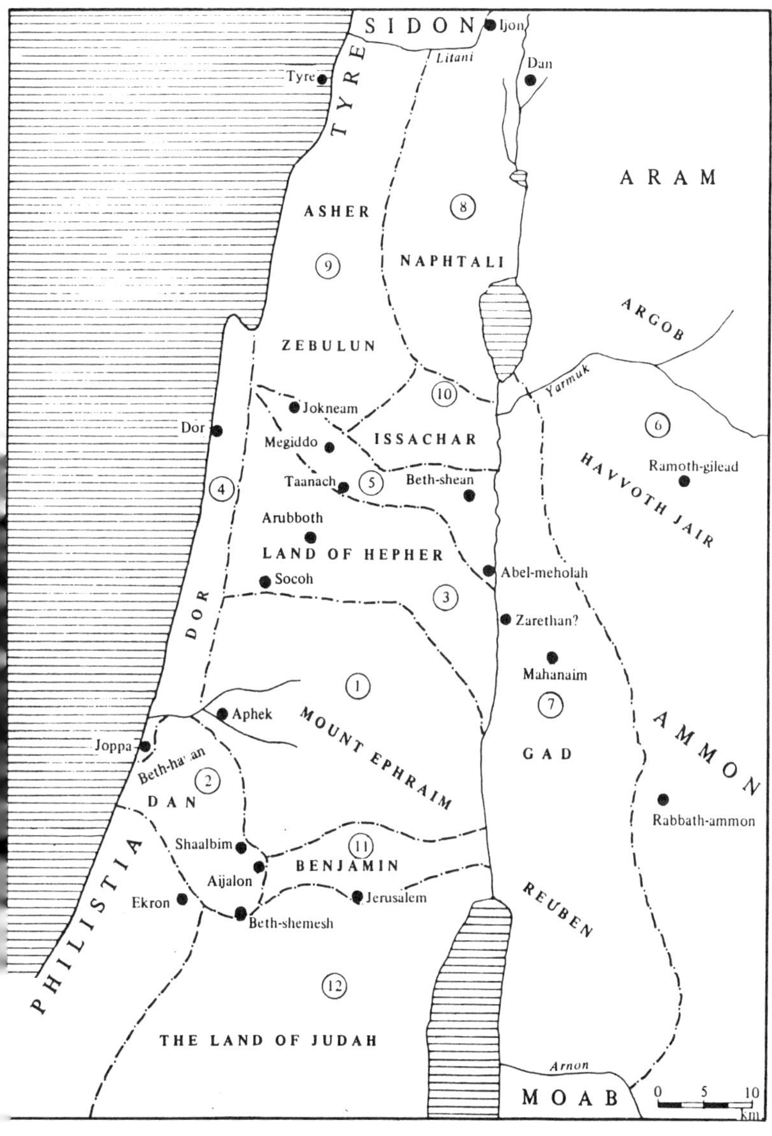

Map 6. The District System.

The fifth district thus encompassed the Canaanite parts of the plains of Jezreel and Beth-shean occupied by David. These were situated between the plain of Acco in the north-west and the central Jordan valley in the south-east, and between the inheritances of Issachar and Zebulun on one side and the nuclear inheritance of Manasseh on the other. This whole area was allotted to Manasseh in the boundary system (Josh. 17:10-11), where it was described only by means of a list of towns and their lands. The writer of the district system demarcated the recently occupied Canaanite territory in a more detailed manner.

The Sixth and Seventh Districts

The description of the sixth district - "Ben-geber, in Ramoth-gilead (he had the villages of Jair the son of Manasseh, which are in Gilead, and he had the region of Argob, which is in Bashan...)" 1 Kings 4:13 - follows the pattern of the third district. First the seat of the governor was mentioned (Ramoth-gilead), then the names of the district's geographical regions, preceded by the word *lw* (to him). These regions are the *ḥwt* (whatever that may mean) of Jair, which are in Gilead, and the Argob, which is in Bashan. The *ḥwt* of Jair was apparently a name of the mountainous areas of the Gilead north of the Jabbok river, and the Argob a name of the Bashan situated north and east of the Gilead. The external boundaries of the two regions cannot be determined. In the interpolated verse 19, "Geber the son of Uri, in the land of Gilead" seems to be a duplication of the sixth district, or an alternative reading of it.

The seventh district is marked by a single place, Mahanaim, which was certainly its centre. Of all the twelve districts, the description of the seventh is the least clear. One may ask why the writer did not complete his description, but left such a fragmentary definition. It is possible that he wanted to stress that all the Israelite parts of Transjordan outside the confines of the sixth district, which he had already described, were included in the seventh, and he was therefore satisfied to mention only the capital. But I prefer another explanation: after the word 'Mahanaim', the description was deliberately truncated by the late writer who interpolated verse 19. The original description of the district system may have contained a supplementary definition of the seventh district (e.g., 'to him was the land of Gad', or 'to him was the Gilead and all the tableland'). One may suggest that the original reading conflicted with the interpolated verse by referring to the same area, and was therefore omitted.

The seventh district most probably comprised the two inheritances of Gad and Reuben, bordering the neighbouring kingdoms of Ammon and Moab on the east and south.

The second part of verse 19a, "...the country of Sihon king of the Amorites and of Og king of Bashan",[32] which

32. Albright, "Divisions", pp. 27, 34-35; Mettinger, *Officials,* pp. 121-122; Montgomery, *Kings,* pp. 121, 125-126; M. Ottosson, *Gilead: Tradition and History,* Coniectanea Biblica, Old Testament Series, vol. 3 (Lund 1969), pp. 217-220. By assuming that there

is obviously out of place [see pp. 174-176], was taken from Deuteronomistic descriptions of Transjordan (cf. in verse 13: "sixty great cities with walls and bronze bars").

The Ninth and Tenth Districts

Three of the Galilean tribes are mentioned by name (Naphtali, Asher and Issachar), and only Zebulun appears to be missing. It has been suggested that the inheritance of Zebulun was included in the district of his southern neighbour, Issachar.[33] This was based on the assumption of a close association between Issachar and Zebulun (Deut. 33:18-19) and the mention of only one tribe where we would have expected to find two (Josh. 17:10; Judg. 6:34-35). The area of Issachar's inheritance was too small to constitute a district on its own, and the tenth district should have included the neighbouring territory of Zebulun.

Other scholars assumed that Zebulun's name must have been recorded and was originally mentioned next to Asher's in 1 Kings 4:16. Since the name *b'lwt* (or *'lwt*) is nowhere else connected with this north-western region, they assumed it to be

were three Transjordanian districts in the system, scholars had great difficulty in interpreting verse 19 (e.g., Kallai, *Tribes*, pp. 60-61; Aharoni, "Solomonic", pp. 11-12).

33. Saarisalo, *Boundary*, p. 95; Herrmann, "Issakar", pp. 23-24; Kallai, *Tribes*, pp. 57-59.

a corruption of Zebulun, and accordingly emended the text to: in Asher and Zebulun.[34] This latter assumption seems to be the more reasonable of the two, since it accounts for all the difficulties inherent in the description of District IX: (a) the absence of the tribe of Zebulun; (b) the appearance of the mysterious name *b'lwt,* which is the only unknown regional or tribal name in the entire district system; (c) the process by which the name *zblwn* was miscopied as *b'lwt.* I tend to accept this emendation until a more convincing solution is put forward.

The appearance of Zebulun and Asher within one district may explain the extremely problematic allusion to Zebulun in Jacob's blessing. Gen. 49:13 "Zebulun shall dwell at the shore of the sea; he shall become a haven for ships, and his border shall be at Sidon". A glance at the borders of the ninth district – situated along the Mediterranean coast and touching on Tyre and Sidon – will make it clear that the poet was referring to this stretch of land, designating it by the name Zebulun.

34. Alt, "Israels Gaue", p. 14 n. 2 [=*KS,* vol. 2, p. 85 n. 1]; Abel, *Géographie,* pp. 80, 82; Wright, "Provinces", p. 59* and n. 8; Mettinger, *Officials,* p. 118; Aharoni, "Solomonic", p. 12. This conjecture was epigraphically supported by Cross (in: Wright, "Provinces", p. 59*). For criticism of this proposal, see Montgomery, *Kings,* p. 126; Kallai, *Tribes,* p. 57; G.W. Ahlstroem, "A Note on a Textual Problem in 1 Kings 4:16", *BASOR,* no. 235 (1979), pp. 79-80.

This, in my opinion, is another indication of the flexibility of tribal geography in ancient Israel, which was quite different from the boundary system as recorded in Josh. 13-19 [cf. pp. 88-95].

The Twelfth District

The end of 1 Kings 4:19, unless it was abridged by a late Judaean writer, must originally have run thus: "...and there was one officer in the land of Judah", and not "in Judah", as was the case in the other tribal districts. I believe that this designation was intended to distinguish the twelfth district from the inheritance of Judah (cf. 'Mount Ephraim' as against 'Ephraim'). The author of the boundary system attached the coast of the Philistines to Judah's allotment (although it was never an integral part of the Israelite kingdom, nor had it anything to do with the tribe's territory), in order to magnify his own tribe, which was also the king's. The author of the district system considered it necessary to define it by the geographical-ethnic designation, "the land of Judah". This is another illustration of the precision with which the list of Solomon's prefects was recorded.

3) Historical Background

The district system in 1 Kings 4:7-19 shows how the basic administrative division of the Israelite kingdom at its peak – the later days of David and the reign of Solomon – was used as an administrative framework for all the needs of the kingdom. The entire system was most probably established by David as an outcome of the census (2 Sam. 24). The results of the census served as a basis for determining the taxes and levies throughout the Israelite kingdom.[35]

In order to improve our understanding of the district system we should compare it with the boundary system. That comparison indicates some identical features, and some marked differences. The fundamental division into territorial blocs – the northern, central and southern tribes west of the Jordan, and the Transjordanian tribes – is common to both. This is not surprising, since they were recorded at roughly the same time. The many differences in detail have already been discussed, but it is important to emphasize the main variations in their respective boundaries. The literary design of the system of tribal allotments – twelve tribes dividing up the entire country with no territorial gap between them – obliged its author to combine actual tribal elements with additions and extensions of non-tribal elements. [See pp. 93-94, 169]. In the district system, on the other hand, these two elements were separated. The district system represents the administrative division of the United Monarchy. But since, as we have already shown, administrative systems were always based on the topography and organizational traditions of a given area, it may tell us something about territorial conditions in the country prior to David's conquests.[36]

35. Albright, *Religion*, pp. 123-124; Kallai, *Tribes*, pp. 245-246.

36. The proposal that the sequence of districts in 1 Kings 4:7-19

Alt, in his seminal study of the district system, emphasized the distinction between districts based on nuclear inheritances designated by the names of tribes (Mount Ephraim, Naphtali, Asher and Zebulun, Issachar, Benjamin, Gad/Gilead), and those based on recently conquered territories of Canaanite city-states, which were designated by lists of towns or names of regions (the cities of Dan, Socoh and the land of Hepher, the region of Dor, the Jezreel and Beth-shean valleys, the *ḥwt* of Jair and the region of Argob, Mahanaim). To quote Alt's own words: "Die Umschreibung der einzelnen Gaugebiete aber ist ganz und gar durch den historischen Charakter der Landschaften bestimmt; Stammesgebiete und Stadtgebiete, letztere wegen ihres geringen Umfanges meistens zu groesseren Komplexen vereinigt, stehen sich hier gegenueber".[37] Alt's view is supported by many scholars.[38]

reflects the gradual expansion of the Israelite kingdom during the time of David (Mazar, "Dan", p. 69 n. 11; Yeivin, op. cit. [see note 19 above], pp. 51-52) has no textual or logical support. Why should one expect to find the chronological order of David's conquests in an administrative list of governors and their districts?

37. Alt, "Israels Gaue", pp. 9-19 (cited from p. 16) [=*KS*, vol. 2, pp. 81-89; cited from p. 87]; cf. Alt, "Landnahme", pp. 9-30 [=*KS*, vol. 1, pp. 97-121].

38. For example, Albright, "Divisions", pp. 17, 31-32; Mettinger, *Officials*, pp. 118-120; Aharoni, "Solomonic", pp. 5-6, 13-14.

We propose to re-examine Alt's differentiation between districts of tribal origin and those of city-state origin, in order to gain a better understanding of the organization and character of the population just before the foundation of the Monarchy.

Since Alt's conclusions were based mainly on his reconstruction of the district system, we must first present the major differences between his delineation of the districts and ours. (a) He proposed that the first district was comprised of the nuclear inheritances of Ephraim and Manasseh, and that the third district should be located only in the Sharon plain. We have suggested that both the first and third districts should be located in the hill country and that they comprised the nuclear inheritances of Ephraim and Manasseh. (b) Alt thought that the area of Transjordan was divided into three districts and that the twelfth district consisted of the inheritances of Gad and Reuben. In our view, the area of Transjordan was divided into two districts only, and the inheritances of Gad and Reuben were included in the seventh district. (c) According to Alt, Judah was not included within the district system. We suggest that it was.

Alt was certainly correct in his assertion that the second and fifth districts were established in the areas of Canaanite city-states, remaining independent entities up to the beginning of the 10th century B.C., and preserving their particular social and cultural character. After their conquest and annexation, they were organized as separate districts. The fourth district was also occupied by non-Israelite groups descended from the 'Sea

Peoples' and regarded by the biblical historiographers as 'Canaanites' (Josh. 17:11-13; Judg. 1:27-28). On the other hand, there were districts in which foreign elements (often called 'Canaanites' or 'Amorites') and Israelite tribal elements lived side by side until the time of the United Monarchy.

The list of Judg. 1:21, 27-35 includes the most important unconquered Canaanite cities west of the Jordan. Alt thought that the list reflected David's conquest of the Canaanite enclaves. However, having dated the original boundary system to the pre-monarchial period, he was obliged to interpret the list of unconquered Canaanite cities, which is in harmony with the inheritances of the tribes, as a kind of fulfilment of the Israelite tribes' theoretical claims on these territories.[39] We, on the other hand, believe that the boundary system reflects the reality of the time of the United Monarchy, and that the list of unconquered Canaanite cities is actually the list of the important non-Israelite cities conquered by David [see chapter 2 pp. 95-98]. Some of these cities were included in the inheritances of Zebulun, Asher and Naphtali. It is therefore evident that the eighth (Naphtali) and ninth (Asher and Zebulun) districts, regarded by Alt as districts of a 'tribal'

39. Alt, "System", pp. 16-19 [=*KS,* vol. 1, pp. 196-198]; id., "Staatenbildung", *KS,* vol. 2, p. 51 n. 1; M. Noth, *Das System der zwoelf Staemme Israels,* BWANT, vol. IV,1 (Stuttgart 1930; reprinted Darmstadt 1966), pp. 129-130; id., *History,* pp. 54 n. 2, 192-193; id., *Josua,* p. 13; Schmitt, *Frieden,* pp. 53-89, and n. 53, with further literature.

nature, were inhabited even as late as David's time by mixed elements of 'Israelites' and 'Canaanites'.

Furthermore, extensive areas in Transjordan were conquered and annexed during the time of the United Monarchy, and in the descriptions of the allotments of the Transjordanian tribes (Reuben, Gad and half of the tribe of Manasseh), the nuclear inheritances of the Israelite tribes were mingled with the recently-conquered foreign elements ('Amorites'). The Transjordanian districts (VI and VII) should also be regarded as 'mixed' districts.

In addition to these four mixed districts – where tribal and 'Canaanite' elements preserving their separate organization and social structure existed side by side as late as David's conquest – there were other so-called Israelite districts in which foreign elements lived alongside the Israelites, and were absorbed in the tribal organization. For example, Manassite families which had settled in the mountains of Samaria, eventually absorbed Canaanite elements, and they were bound to influence each other.[40] It was not mere chance that the early capital cities of the northern Israelite kingdom were situated in the main Canaanite centres of Shechem and Tirzah, and that the Canaanite elements acquired special influence in the

40. A. Alt, "Erwaegungen ueber die Landnahme der Israeliten in Palaestina", *PJb*, vol. 35 (1939), pp. 9-12 [=*KS*, vol. 1, pp. 127-129]; id., "Meros", *ZAW*, vol. 58 (1941), p. 246 [=*KS*, vol. 1, p. 275].

kingdom throughout the monarchial period.[41] There was a Hivite enclave in the inheritance of Benjamin until the time of the United Monarchy; the Jebusite city of Jerusalem, first conquered by David, was situated on its southern side. The tribe of Judah was formed from sections of mixed origin, including 'Canaanite' elements in the Shephelah region (Gen. 38). Its distinct 'Israelite' identity seems to have taken definite shape only under David.[42]

In light of all this we may conclude that the ethnic, social and cultural picture of the different regions of the new kingdom at the time of David and Solomon was a variegated one, and that the biblical distinction between 'Israelites' and 'Canaanites' does not fully reflect the complexity of the situation during the United Monarchy.

41. For the place of the Canaanite elements in the history of Israel during the monarchial period, see Alt, "Stadtstaat". Alt's presentation of the duality of the Israelite and Canaanite elements in the Northern Kingdom and of Samaria as the 'Canaanite' capital of the kingdom is not acceptable. Nevertheless, his emphasis on the strong Canaanite influence on the Northern Kingdom as a result of the survival of Canaanite elements within the inheritance of Manasseh is justified and helps to clarify the historical picture. See the discussion of the personal names of the Samaria Ostraca by Lemaire, *Inscriptions*, pp. 55, 76.

42. De Vaux, *Early History*, pp. 523-550.

Alt's fundamental assumption that the division into districts was based mainly upon the existing structure of the recently-conquered and annexed territories of the Israelite kingdom is acceptable. The administration of the tribal districts remained virtually unchanged in those areas where there was tribal unity prior to the foundation of the monarchy (Districts I, III, X, XI). It should, however, be emphasized that this tribal organization may have encompassed foreign as well as Israelite elements. Other areas, recently conquered and with long-established patterns of government, society and culture, were organized in separate distrcits (II, IV, and V). Nevertheless, there were several regions where Israelite groups and foreign elements had to be combined within the confines of a single district (VI, VII, VIII, IX, and XII).

We may conclude that geographical, political, and administrative divisions entrenched for many generations combined to dictate the fashioning of the district system established by David. Despite the considerable changes in the borders during the time of the United Monarchy, the district system seems to have survived, though on a reduced scale, as the basic administrative system of the Northern and Southern Kingdoms until their final destruction.

CHAPTER SIX

A NEW LOOK AT THE SYSTEM OF LEVITICAL CITIES

1) History of Research

The system of Levitical cities has come down to us in two documents (Josh. 21; 1 Chr. 6:54-81 [= MT 6:39-66]), each belonging to a composition having a different focus of interest. In the book of Joshua, the system follows the description of the tribal inheritances. In the book of Chronicles, it appears in the genealogical lists of the Israelite tribes, and is connected to the tribe of Levi.

The system allocates 48 cities from among the twelve tribes of Israel to the four main Levite families: Aaronites, the rest of the Kohathites, Gershonites and Merarites. The historicity of the system has long been debated, and the pattern of its geographical distribution as well as its contribution to the understanding of the history of the priesthood in Israel have been discussed many times.[1] Several scholars have regarded the

1. See, Albright, "Levitic"; Noth, *Josua*, pp. 127-132; Alt, "Judaeischen Ortslisten"; Mazar, "Levites"; Haran, "Studies"; id., *Temples*, pp. 112-131; de Vaux, *Ancient Israel*, pp. 366-367; Aharoni, *LB*, pp. 269-273; Kallai, *Tribes*, pp. 377-403; id., "System"; Mettigner, *Officials*, pp. 98-101; Auld, "Levitical". For

system as a plan conceived in either the early days of the Israelite settlement in Canaan,[2] or in a very late period, after the Babylonian captivity, but never put into operation.[3] Others, however, have regarded the system, or certain elements of it, as reflecting the reality of a particular period. But they disagree as to which were the older parts and which were the later expansions. Some regarded the territorial distribution of the 48 cities among the tribes as the original part, the four Levite families as a later addition;[4] others thought the process was exactly the other way round.[5]

a more detailed list of literature see Helga Weippert, "Das geographische System der Staemme Israels", *VT*, vol. 23 (1973), p. 83 n. 1; Haran, *Temples*, p. 113 n. 3.

2. Y. Kaufmann, *The Biblical Account of the Conquest of Palestine* [see above p. 35 note 4], pp. 40-46.

3. J. Wellhausen, *Prolegomena zur Geschichte Israels*, sixth edition (Leipzig 1927), pp. 153-158; [English translation: *Prolegomena to the History of Ancient Israel* (New York 1957)]; H.W. Hertzberg, *Die Buecher Josua, Richter, Ruth, ATD* vol. 9 (Goettingen 1959), pp. 118-120; Mowinckel, *Tetrateuch*, pp. 71-73; Auld, "Levitical".

4. J. Liver, *Chapters in the History of the Priests and Levites: Studies in the Lists of Chronicles and Ezra and Nehemiah* (Jerusalem 1968), p. 30 n. 74 [Hebrew]; Kallai, "System", pp. 20-28.

5. Noth, *Josua*, p. 127.

When trying to date and understand the system, scholars naturally took the town list as an Archimedian point. The position and date of office of the four Levite families can only be resolved by literary analysis, the results of which are extremely controversial. On the other hand, the historical as well as administrative setting of the town list can be established by comparison with other biblical documents, and the results of geographical and archaeological research. Several discussions have been devoted to establishing the correct text of the town names and locating them within the tribal inheritances. By determining the borders of the kingdom and the location of the cities, scholars hoped to date the entire complex and to understand the historical significance of the system.

These studies led to a clear-cut conclusion: that the town list dates to the United Monarchy. Only in this period were all these towns under Israelite rule: some of them were not under Israelite control either before the reign of David or after the reign of Solomon.[6] Some of the scholars supporting this view have even used the list of Levitical cities as a basis for

6. A different solution was proposed by Alt ("Judaeische Ortslisten", pp. 199-206 [=*KS*, vol. 2, pp. 294-301]), who combined the distribution of the Levitical cities with the cultic reform of Josiah. But even he had to admit that the author of the system of Levitical cities had before him an earlier document. Nevertheless, he maintained that both this and the other literary stages reflected in the system should be dated to a time shortly before Josiah (ibid., p. 206).

discussions of various problems connected with the time of the United Monarchy.[7]

Regarding the meaning of the term 'Levitical cities', Mazar suggested that they were administrative and cultic centres in which Levites were settled by the royal court of Jerusalem.[8] He proposed that the Levites were dispatched to various centres throughout the country "...for everything pertaining to God and for the affairs of the king" (1 Chr. 26:32), and explained the distribution of Levitical cities, located mainly in the peripheral areas and the Canaanite enclaves of the kingdom, as resulting from this policy. According to Mazar, the cities were key points selected all over the kingdom in order to unite and consolidate the newly-conquered territories.[9]

However, further examination of the data indicates that the historical reliability of the system is not well established. The historicity of the scheme of 48 cities, four from each of the 12 tribes, which has long been suspect,

7. This is conspicuous in the work of Kallai (*Tribes*, pp. 127, 132-133, 154-156, 262, 266-268).

8. Mazar, "Levites", pp. 196-202.

9. Mazar's explanation of the system was accepted by Aharoni, *LB*, pp. 269-273; Kallai, "System", p. 25; cf. B. Halpern, "Levitic Participation in the Reform Cult of Jeroboam I", *JBL*, vol. 95 (1976), pp. 34-35.

remains doubtful. Moreover, the basic assumption that the entire Israelite territory was actually divided among the 12 tribes is questionable. Those who argue in favour of the historicity of the equal division of the Levitical cities among the 12 tribes would first have to prove that the kingdom's territory on both sides of the Jordan was in fact divided into 12 administrative units, named after the Israelite tribes.

In chapter 2 we have tried to demonstrate that the system of twelve tribes originated as a 'literary' document in the comprehensive composition describing the period of the occupation and settlement of the land by the Israelites, and that the boundary system was never used as the basis of an administration. By interpreting the boundary system as a purely literary historiographic composition, we refute the actuality of the division of the land into twelve allotments, and thus invalidate the assumption that the list of Levitical cities was connected with the administration of the country.

The period of the Monarchy cannot possibly be the background of the system for another reason: many cult centres of that time are not included among the Levitical cities. While the omission of Jerusalem as the capital is understandable, the absence of cities like Dan, Bethel, Mizpah Gilgal, Bethlehem, Beer-sheba, Arad, Nebo and Ataroth (see the Mesha stele) is surprising. Haran has tried to account for this by making a distinction between 'shrine cities' and 'Levitical cities'. In his opinion, shrine cities contained a house of God where a regular cult was practised, whereas Levitical cities were residential centres of the Levites and their families.[10]

However, even if the two designations were not identical, one would still expect to find Levites living in the main shrine cities. In Israel, as in all other ancient Near Eastern kingdoms, the centres of government and administration were also the main cultic centres. The absence of important administrative and cultic centres such as Dan, Bethel and Beer-sheba from the list does not accord with the explanations of the system offered until now.[11] It is a strong argument against the assertion that the 48 towns are an authentic element in a document from the time of the Monarchy.

10. Haran, "Studies", pp. 48-53 [=*Temples,* pp. 116-122]; Kallai, *Tribes,* p. 386.

11. Haran ("Studies", pp. 51-53) suggests that the priests did not live and function in the same place. As an example he argued that the priests of the House of Eli originally served at Shiloh and, following its destruction, moved to Nob, while their families lived at Anathoth. However, Shiloh was destroyed in the days of Eli and its priests moved to other places, including Nob and Anathoth. Furthermore, Nob is specifically called "the city of the priests" (1 Sam. 22:19) being a place of both cult and residence for themselves and their families. Haran's separation seems artificial. It is more likely that the families of the Levites lived in the cult cities but also had fields and pasture lands in other places.

2) The Texts of Joshua 21 and 1 Chronicles 6

The entire system of Levitical cities in Josh. 21, containing 48 cities distributed among the twelve tribes and four Levite families, is a uniform literary unit. This unit consists of four main parts: (a) a short introduction (vv. 1-3); (b) a list of 48 cities distributed among twelve tribes; (c) verses relating to the six cities of refuge; (d) a series of passages introducing and summarizing the division of 48 cities among the four Levite families (vv. 9-10, 19-20, 26-27, 33-34, 40-41 [= MT 38-39]). The discernment of original and secondary elements in the system of Levitical cities is, in my opinion, not well founded. Both the claim that the four Levite families are original and the distribution of the 48 cities among the 12 tribes secondary, and the claim that the 'map' of tribes and cities is original, and the division among the Levite families secondary, are based on a priori assumptions rather than on literary analysis of the text. It is obvious that any division of 48 cities among twelve tribes and four families must have been schematic, but this in itself does not prove the secondary character or the late date of either of them.

In spite of the list being a uniform literary unit, there are some secondary additions to the text of Josh. 21, such as the summaries of the tribes (16b, 18b, 22b, 24b, 25b, etc.), which are missing from the list of 1 Chr. 6. They were therefore added to the text of Joshua at a later stage, after the Chronicler had copied the list from Joshua. [Further examples are given below]. Verses 4-7 may also be a late addition to the text of

Joshua, as suggested by the *Wiederaufnahme* in verse 8a of verse 3a (*wytnw bny yśr'l llwym*);[12] but verses 4-7 were clearly incorporated into the text of Joshua prior to the Chronicler's editing of the text (cf. 1 Chr. 6:61-63 [= MT 6:46-48]). The original system of Levitical cities, with its four main parts, was, however, composed at one time by a single writer according to a definite literary and historiographic plan.

Auld has examined the relation of the two texts of the system of Levitical cities in Josh. 21 and 1 Chr. 6.[13] He first presents the texts, and then compares them. He demonstrates that the text of 1 Chr. 6 consists of two major parts: the list of Aaronite cities (vv. 54-60 [=MT 39-45]) and the list of Levitical cities, divided among the Levite families (vv. 61-81 [=MT 46-66]). He then argues that 1 Chr. 6 developed in several stages and that its nucleus was the list of 13 Aaronite cities in the tribal areas of Judah, Simeon and Benjamin. The more elaborate and harmonious arrangement of the material in Josh. 21 is explained as a result of later editing of the text of Chronicles.

Auld's contention about the originality of the text of 1 Chr. 6, and the secondary nature and late date of Josh. 21 is not convincing. In the first place, his basic claim about the growth in stages of the text of 1 Chr. 6 is not plausible, as the geographical scope of both the 13 Aaronite cities and the

12. Noth, *Josua*, p. 127.

13. Auld, "Levitical".

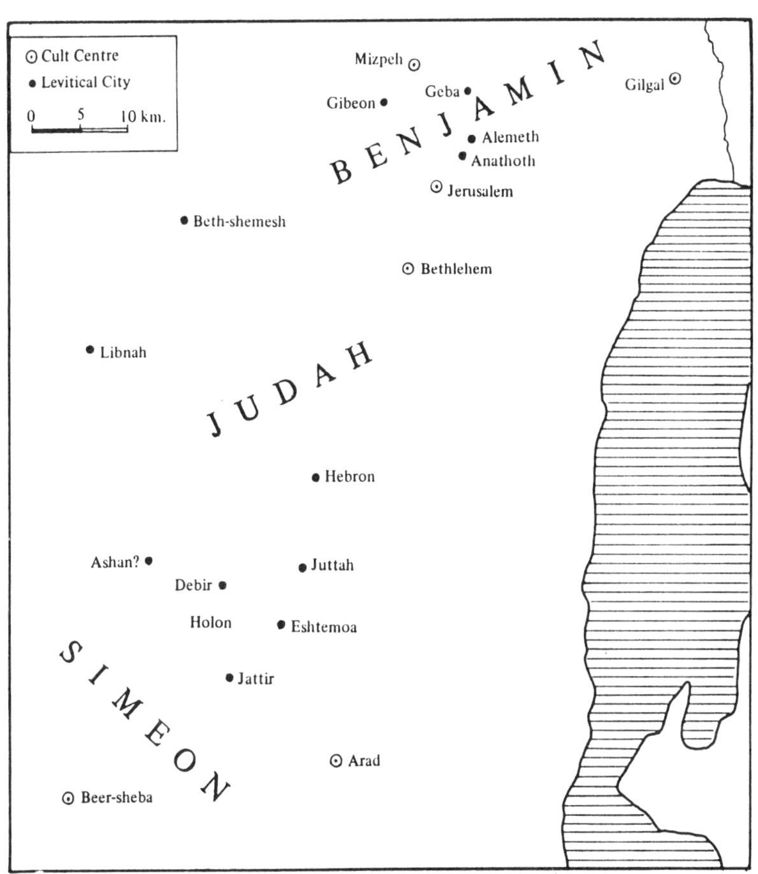

Map 7. Levitical Cities – Kingdom of Judah.

48 Levitical cities fits the reality of the time of the Monarchy, but not that of the period in which Chronicles was compiled. Since no part of the list reflects the reality of the period of the Chronicler, it is odd to assume that this document was compiled in several stages at such a late date. It is more reasonable to suppose that the literary form of the chapter in 1 Chr. 6 is due to the Chronicler's elaboration of the source he had before him – the system of Levitical cities of Josh. 21 – which he edited according to his own historiographic principles.

The Chronicler's accentuation of the designation 'Aaronites' (nowhere are they called priests or Levites) is due to his distinction between the Levites (1 Chr. 6:48[=MT 6:33]) and the Aaronites (1 Chr. 6:49 [= MT 6:34]). After the genealogy of the Aaronite families (1 Chr. 6:50-53 [= MT 6:35-38]) he added a short introductory note (v. 54a [= MT 39a]) and then copied, with minor alterations, Josh. 21:10-19, enumerating the cities of the Aaronites (1 Chr. 6:54b-60 [= MT 6:39b-45]). Having completed the section dealing with the Aaronites (1 Chr. 6:49-60 [= MT 6:34-45]), he went on to copy the other parts of the list in Joshua.

We shall not enter into a detailed discussion of all the arguments raised by Auld, but some comments are required.

Neither the introduction in Joshua (21:1-3), nor the following verse (4), was relevant to the work of the Chronicler, who therefore omitted them and began copying only from

Josh. 21:11.[14] As a result, the text of 1 Chr. 6 is somewhat obscure regarding the question of who is allotting the towns to the Aaronites (vv. 55, 56, 57 [= MT 40, 41, 42]). The answer is to be found in the text of Josh 21, which, to my mind, is the earlier of the two, and where it is explicitly stated that Eleazar the priest, Joshua, and the heads of the tribes of Israel allocated the cities to the Levites.

Auld assumed the precedence of the text of 1 Chr. 6 on the basis of "the general tendency of texts to grow and accrete", since in several instances the text of Joshua is more detailed.[15] In the case of the term 'Levites', however, it is clear that it was deliberately omitted by the scribe of 1 Chr. 6. The text of verse 71 [= MT 56]: "To the Gershomites *mmšpḥt* [RSV: were given out of] the half-tribe of Manasseh...", is an anomaly, since only the Levites appear in this chapter as 'families' (*mšpḥwt*). A comparison with the text of Josh. 21:27 ("And to the Gershonites, one of the families of the Levites, were given out of the half-tribe of Manasseh...") immediately shows the anomaly to be the result of the removal of the word 'Levites' by the Chronicler. Furthermore, verse 77 [= MT 62] "to the rest of the Merarites" is also obscure, since nothing has

14. Noth, *Josua*, p. 127. The author of 1 Chr. 6 opened his description with the 13 Aaronite cities (vv. 54b-60 [= MT 6:39b-45]) and continued with the Levitical summary (vv. 61-64 [= MT 6:46-49]). This reversal of the order of the two sections in Josh. 21, made verse 4 superfluous and it was therefore omitted by the Chronicler.

15. Auld, "Levitical", p. 198.

been said previously about the other sons of Merari. The comparison with Josh. 21:34 ("And to the rest of the Levites, the Merarite families...") immediately explains this anomaly.

In other cases, the text of Josh. 21 seems to have expanded by additions and alterations only after the text of 1 Chr. 6 was compiled.[16] A clear example is Josh. 21:16b: "nine cities out of these two tribes". Not only has the verse no parallel in 1 Chr. 6, but the word *šbṭ* is alien to both chapters, *mṭh* being used throughout. Another example is the individual tribal summaries, which are one of the secondary elements in the late editing of the text of Joshua, and are entirely missing in the text of 1 Chr. 6.

1 Chr. 6:65 [= MT 6:50] poses a special problem. This verse is out of keeping with the rest of the chapter, and Auld's contention that it is "a pedantic note" as well as a stage in the development of the text is not convincing.[17] To begin with, this is the only time the compound *mṭh bny*, which is common in Joshua, appears in the entire book of Chronicles. Also, the tribe of Simeon is altogether out of place in this verse in Chronicles, since in the detailed description in verses 55-59

16. For the gradual enlargement of the text of Joshua during the late stages of its editing, see A.G. Auld, "Textual and Literary Studies in the Book of Joshua", *ZAW*, vol. 90 (1978), pp. 412-417; id., "Joshua: The Hebrew and Greek Texts", *SVT*, vol. 30 (1979), pp. 1-14.

17. Auld, "Levitical", p. 196.

[=MT 40-44], only the land of Judah is mentioned. Verse 65 [=MT 50] can therefore only be explained as a copy of the text of Josh. 21:9, since in Joshua, Simeon appears with Judah all along (Josh. 21:4, 9). This verse (65 [=MT 50]), however, was transferred by the Chronicler after the list of Aaronite cities (vv. 54-60 [=MT 39-45]) and the summary of the tribes which made allotments to the three Levite families (vv. 61-64 [=MT 46-49]), and thus removed from its original context.[18]

Further, it should be noted that the noun *mṭh* is common in the book of Joshua, while in Chronicles it appears only twice: once in our chapter and once in 1 Chr. 12:31. It was certainly taken from the text of Joshua.[19]

To sum up, there are many indications that Josh. 21 in its primary form is the earlier text and that the text of 1 Chr. 6:54-81 [=MT 39-66] is dependent upon it.

18. The words *mmṭh bny bnymn* most probably existed in the original text of Josh. 21:9 and were mistakenly omitted during the process of transmission. This is supported by some MSS of the LXX as well as by the parallel verse in 1 Chr. 6:65 and the closely-related text of Josh. 21:4.

19. Josh. 21:2, 3, 26, 33, 41 [= MT 39], 42 [= MT 40] are missing in the parallel text of 1 Chr. 6. Therefore contrary to Auld ("Levitical" p. 198) the absence of *mgršym* (pasture land) should not be discussed in isolation; the entire verse should be considered.

Nevertheless, Auld's observation that the 13 Aaronite cities located within the borders of the kingdom of Judah reflect the earliest, original part of the document is convincing. The exceptional allocation of the nine cities to the tribe of Judah (including Simeon) has the ring of authenticity. But one must certainly reject the proposal that Beth-shemesh, one of the cities of Judah, should be transferred to Naphtali in order to create a harmonious list.[20] This irregular number 13 is an important consideration in our re-evaluation of the system of Levitical cities.

3) The List of Levitical Cities

The perfect accord between the list of Levitical cities and the extent of the kingdom of David and Solomon, as determined by historical, topographical and archaeological research, was not discussed by Auld. It seems to have been the reason for earlier scholars dating the list to the time of the United Monarchy. There is, however, another possible interpretation. A writer living in a late period could have made use of an early, authentic document from which he selected the names of towns for inclusion in his composition of Levitical cities. The pattern of towns in such a text could be identical to that of the early document from which he drew his data. Yet the complete system of cities would still lack any historical significance either in the early period or in his own time.

20. Y. Tsafrir, "The Levitic City of Beth-shemesh in Judah or in Naphtali?", *Eretz Israel,* vol. 12 (1975), pp. 44-45 [Hebrew].

It is our purpose to demonstrate that the system of Levitical cities was compiled in just this manner. The author's point of departure was the 13 Aaronite cities of the kingdom of Judah, within the territory of the three tribes: Judah, Simeon and Benjamin. In his effort to transform this 'Judaean system' into an all-Israelite system according to his schematic design for the work – 48 cities, four per tribe, divided among four Levite families – he made use of the list of tribal inheritances (Josh. 13-19). To his list of towns he added the six cities of refuge situated on both sides of the Jordan. Since the list of tribal inheritances reflects the period of the United Monarchy, all the towns 'borrowed' from it must have flourished at that time. But the complete system of Levitical cities has no historical significance whatever; it is only the list of 13 Aaronite cities in the kingdom of Judah that reflects historical reality.[21]

It would seem that the author first integrated into his system the six cities of refuge, which according to the Priestly Code were connected with the office of priest. Then, in order to give the maximum credibility to his composition, he selected well-known towns from other geographical lists and from the

21. For the borrowing of toponyms by the Pharaohs from the topographical lists of their predecessors, see R. Giveon, "Remarks on the Transmission of Egyptian Lists of Asiatic Toponyms", in: *Fragen an die altaegyptische Literatur: Studien zum Gedenken an E. Otto*, eds. J. Assmann et alii (Wiesbaden 1977), pp. 171-183.

tribal inheritances. Since three tribes were located in Transjordan, the three cities of refuge east of the river were divided among them. The 13 original cities of the Aaronites were necessarily recorded in the territory of the kingdom of Judah, and thus filled the quota of the three tribes. This explains the omission of cities such as Beer-sheba, Arad, Bethlehem and Mizpah, inhabited by Levites descended from non-Aaronite families.

In the other tribal areas, the writer based himself exclusively on the descriptions of the tribal inheritances and the cities of refuge, and left out cities such as Dan, Gilgal and Nebo, which were not mentioned in these sources. It is possible that Bethel, although mentioned in the boundary system, was ignored because of the hatred its name aroused in the court of Jerusalem, on account of the deep rivalry between the two main cult centres of Judah and Israel. The proposed procedure of 'borrowing' thus explains one of the main puzzles: the absence from the system of Levitical cities of well-known cult centres dating to the time of the Monarchy.

The list of Levitical cities in Chronicles differs slightly from the list in Joshua: (a) there are only 42, as against 48 in Joshua; (b) the order is slightly different; (c) there are variations in the form of some names.

As was shown above, the list of Joshua 21 is earlier than, and formed the basis of, 1 Chr. 6. Thus the list of 48 cities, four per tribe, is part of the original composition, and

Albright was right in asserting that the texts of Joshua and Chronicles are based on a uniform list of towns.[22] The discussion below, in which we point out the close connection between names in the list of Levitical cities and in the tribal inheritances, is founded mainly on Albright's textual analysis of the city names. We try to show how the author composed his list of towns and to explain certain contradictions between the boundary system and the system of Levitical cities.

a) Reuben [23]

The names of the three cities (Jahaz, Kedemoth and Mephaath) appear together and in that order in the description of Reuben's inheritance (Josh. 13:18) and were copied directly by our writer. To this trio he added the city of refuge, Bezer. The list of Reubenite Levitical cities is the only example of straight copying from the tribal inheritances.

b) Gad [24]

Mahanaim, Heshbon and Jaazer are mentioned in the description of the inheritance of Gad, though in a slightly different order (Josh. 13:25-27). As the fourth town, the writer included the refuge city of Ramoth-gilead.

22. Albright, "Levitic", pp. 51-55.

23. Josh. 21:36-37 [RSV]; 1 Chr. 6:78-79 [= MT 6:63-64].

24. Josh. 21:38-39 [= MT 21:36-37]; 1 Chr. 6:80-81 [= MT 6:65-66].

A comparison with the tribal inheritances shows that a double mistake occurred. Although Heshbon is mentioned in the boundary description of Gad (Josh. 13:26), it clearly belonged to the territory of Reuben (Josh. 13:17). It was attached to the wrong tribe by the writer, who was not fully acquainted with the precise territorial delineations.[25] According to the boundary system, on the other hand, Ramoth-gilead was located in Manasseh.[26] But since the scribe wished to divide the three cities of refuge among the three Transjordanian tribes, he assigned it to Gad.

c) Manasseh[27]

Only two cities, Ashtaroth and Edrei, are mentioned in the eastern part of Manasseh's inheritance (Josh. 13:31). The writer selected the better-known of the two, Ashtaroth, adding the third Transjordanian city of refuge, Golan. Only a few cities were available to the writer in the western part of Manasseh, since its inheritance includes only a boundary description and no list of towns. For the western half of Manasseh, therefore, he selected Taanach and Ibleam, in the north of the inheritance (Josh. 17:11; cf. Judg. 1:27), as representative towns.

25. Albright, *Religion*, pp. 122-123; Kallai, *Tribes*, pp. 266-268.

26. Kallai, *Tribes*, pp. 266-268.

27. Josh. 21:25, 27; 1 Chr. 6:70-71 [= MT 6:55-56].

d) Ephraim[28]

As with its northern neighbour, there was no list of towns for Ephraim and the writer had only the limited selection mentioned in the boundary description. He chose Gezer and Beth-horon (Josh. 16:3, 5, 10) and added either Kibzaim (Josh. 21:22) or Jokmeam (1 Chr. 6:68 [= MT 6:53]), the location of neither of which is known.[29] Jokmeam and Kibzaim are the only towns whose inclusion in the list of Levitical cities we cannot explain satisfactorily, unless we assume that the description of Ephraim's inheritance was more detailed when the system was composed than it is today.[30]

28. Josh. 21:20-22; 1 Chr. 6:66-68 [= MT 6:51-53].

29. For the names Kibzaim and Jokmeam and their textual affinities, see Albright, "Levitic", pp. 55, 62, 67-68; Mazar, "Levites", p. 198; Kallai, *Tribes*, pp. 137-138, 398; S. Yeivin, "Kibzaim", *EM*, vol. 7 (1976), pp. 1-3 [Hebrew], with further literature. In my view, the Levitical city Jokmeam should be distinguished from the Jokmeam mentioned in the Solomonic district system (1 Kings 4:12). The southern boundary of the fifth Solomonic district reached as far as Abel-meholah (Tell Abu Ṣuṣ), south of the valley of Beth-shean and far beyond the northern boundary of Ephraim. Furthermore, Albright's restoration of 1 Kings 4:12 ("Taanach and Megiddo as far as beyond Yokneam..."), proposing to read Jokneam instead of Jokmeam, is convincing (see Albright, "Divisions" p. 26 n. 19). See also above pp. 187-190.

30. There are indications that the descriptions of the boundaries of Ephraim and Manasseh suffered some mutiliation. The opening verse of the description of Ephraim's northern border (Josh. 16:6

The fourth city of Ephraim is the refuge city of Shechem. Here, too, there is a contradiction between the tribal inheritances and the system of Levitical cities. The boundary of Manasseh was drawn from "Michmethath, which is east of *('l pny)* Shechem" (Josh. 17:7), running southward towards Tappuah. Shechem no doubt belonged to Manasseh's, and not Ephraim's, inheritance. [For a detailed discussion, see chapter 4 pp. 151-153]. The author of the system of Levitical cities who had already assigned one refuge city, Golan, to Manasseh, necessarily assigned the other, Shechem, to Ephraim. It should also be noted that Shechem lay in the geographical region of Mount Ephraim (see Josh. 20:7; 1 Kings 12:25; cf. LXX in 1 Kings 12:24o). This may have influenced the writer to allocate it erroneously, and he may even have regarded it as necessary to support it by quoting "Shechem... in the hill country of Ephraim" (Josh. 21:21).[31]

hmkmtt mṣpwn) was cut. A whole section between Michmethath and Tappuah is missing, as is the entire section between Michmethath and the Jordan in the description of Manasseh's southern boundary. The eastern border of Manaaseh is also missing and the northern border is only briefly described (Josh. 17:11). Admittedly, nothing is known about the early history of the text, nor do we know whether the writers at the time of Josiah had a better-preserved text from which to work.

31. This is contrary to A.G. Auld ("Cities of Refuge in Israelite Tradition", *JSOT,* no. 10 (1978), pp. 32-37), who proposed that in Josh. 21:21 the shorter text of the LXX, without *bhr 'prym* should be followed. But the combination "Shechem... in the hill

e) Dan[32]

All four Levitical cities (Eltekeh, Gibbethon, Aijalon and Gath-rimmon) are also mentioned in the inheritance of Dan (Josh. 19:42-44), in almost the same order.

f) Issachar[33]

In the inheritance of Issachar, all four Levitical cities (Kishion, Daberath, Jarmuth/Ramoth and En-gannim) appear (Josh. 19: 20-21),[34] in nearly the same sequence.

country of Ephraim" is repeated in all descriptions of the refuge cities (Josh. 20:7; 21:21; 1 Chr. 6:67 [= MT 6:52]) and should be preferred. I believe that the author of the system of Levitical cities deliberately added this description to support his erroneous allocation of the city of Shechem to the inheritance of Ephraim.

32. Josh. 21 23-24; 1 Chr. 6:69 [= MT 6:54]. Of the four Levitical cities of Dan mentioned in Josh. 21:23-24, two – Eltekeh and Gibbethon – are missing from 1 Chr. 6 altogether, and the other two – Aijalon and Gath-rimmon – are ascribed to Ephraim.

33. Josh. 21:28-29; 1 Chr. 6:72-73 [= MT 6:57-58].

34. The name of the city of Daberath was mistakenly copied as Rabbith in the list of towns of Issachar (Josh. 19:20). The LXX, however, preserved the correct form. See, A.F. Rainey, "Rabbith, ha-Rabbith", *EM,* vol. 7 (1976), pp. 319-320 [Hebrew], with further literature.

g) Zebulun[35]

Jokneam, Kartah/Tabor, Rimmon and Nahalal are the four Levitical cities of Zebulun. A comparison with the description of the tribal inheritance suggests that the name Tabor is the original, and Kartah a corruption. Tabor is probably a shortened form of the name Chisloth-tabor (Josh. 19:12), although this is by no means certain.[36] If this is correct the four towns of Zebulun in our list are in the same order as in the border description (Josh. 19:11-15).

The city of Jokneam actually belonged to the inheritance of Manasseh and not Zebulun (Josh. 19:11 "...and touches Dabbesheth, then the brook which is *'l pny*[37] Jokneam"). Evidently the writer misunderstood the preposition *'l pny,* to include Jokneam in the inheritance of Zebulun.

In chapter 3 [above pp. 135-138] it was suggested that the name *rmwn* is a metathesis of *mrwn* and that it be identified

35. Josh. 21:34-35; 1 Chr. 6:77 [= MT 6:62].

36. For the textual relations of the two place-names Kartah and Tabor, see Albright, "Levitic", pp. 64-65, 72-73; Kallai, *Tribes,* pp. 401-402. Another possibility is to regard either the Levitical city of *qrth* (Josh. 21:34) or the Zebulunite town of *qṭt* (Josh. 19:15) as a spelling mistake, and to decide for oneself, which is correct.

37. Translated by RSV as 'east of', but would preferably be rendered 'opposite'.

with the city of Marom/Maron (Josh. 11:1; 12:19), which is located in Tel Qarnei Hittin. It thus appears that the writer copied a name which had already been erroneously transcribed in Josh. 19.

h) Asher[38]

All four Levitical cities (Mishal, Abdon, Helkath and Rehob) appear within the inheritance of Asher (Josh. 19:25-28), although in a different order.

i) Naphtali[39]

Since the list of Judah, Simeon and Benjamin included 13 cities, instead of the usual 12, there was a shortage of one city, and Naphtali received only three instead of four. Noth's proposal that, in addition to the refuge city of Kedesh-naphtali, the original version of the list included Hammath and Rakkath (cf. Josh. 19:35), is plausible.[40] The names were also confused during transmission.

To conclude this section on the system of Levitical cities, it seems clear that its form was designed by the author. The 13 original Aaronite cities, situated in the kingdom of Judah, obliged him in one case to deviate from his scheme

38. Josh. 21:30-31; 1 Chr. 6:74-75 [= MT 6:59-60].

39. Josh. 21:32; 1 Chr. 6:76 [= MT 6:61].

40. Noth, *Josua*, pp. 126, 129.

and assign only three towns to a tribe. Two geographical errors occurred in the attribution of cities to tribes because of the incorporation of the cities of refuge within the system (Ramoth-gilead and Shechem). Other mistakes were a result of the writer's erroneous interpretation of the descriptions of the tribal inheritances (Heshbon and Jokneam), or were even due to an earlier mistake in the text of Joshua (Rimmon). Only once did the writer copy a list of towns exactly from the tribal inheritances (Reuben); otherwise he selected the cities at random. In some cases, the original order of the towns selected was maintained, while in others it was changed.

Once it is understood that the system of Levitical cities is based on the boundary system of the twelve tribes, the distribution of the Levitical cities is easily explained. Several towns were taken from the boundary description, and were therefore situated on the borders of the inheritances. In the inheritances of two tribes west of the Jordan, Ephraim and Manasseh, no city lists were available and the writer was therefore obliged to use towns mentioned in the boundary descriptions. This resulted in an enormous territorial gap, which included the mountains of Samaria and the coastal strip. Moreover, Manasseh, occupying a large area on both sides of the Jordan, was considered a single tribe and was accordingly allotted only four towns. Thus the territorial gap in the centre of the country became even larger. Some Levitical towns were Canaanite cities extracted from the town lists and were only annexed to Israelite territory at a late stage.

It is for all these reasons that scholars connected the Levitical cities to the periphery and to the former Canaanite areas of the Israelite kingdom, drawing the erroneous conclusion that the Levites and the Levitical cities played an important part in the unification and integration of the young kingdom in the days of David and Solomon.[41]

4) The Historicity of the System of Levitical Cities

The major contribution of the study of the system to historical research, is the evidence of Aaronite settlements within the kingdom of Judah in the monarchial period.

According to the interpretation proposed above, the commonly-held view of the system of Levitical cities as dating to the time of the United Monarchy is not acceptable. Important for our study is the discussion of Alt, who, although dealing with the system as a uniform document, devoted special attention to the Levitical cities in the kingdom of Judah.[42] He compared the cities recorded in the province list of Judah (Josh. 15:21-62; 18:21-28) with the 13 Aaronite cities, and favoured the dating of both to the time of Josiah (639-609 B.C.). He even went one step further, and tried to

41. Mazar, "Levites", pp. 196-204.

42. Alt, "Judaeische Ortslisten", pp. 199-206 [=*KS*, vol. 2 pp. 294-301].

show that there is a close connection between the distribution of the Levitical cities and the administrative-cultic reform of Josiah. But since the location of the Levitical cities and Josiah's reform did not match exactly, he assumed that the Levitical town list reflects an intermediate stage in the king's activity. Noth, on the other hand, suggested that the system reflects the places outside of Jerusalem where the Levites lived after the time of Josiah. He attributed the existence of Levitical cities in this late period to the incomplete nature of Josiah's administrative-cultic reform.[43]

The first step in the historical inquiry into the Aaronite cities should be an attempt to establish their date. Eight of the nine cities located within the confines of Judah and Simeon are mentioned in the province list of Judah (Josh. 15:21-62), only Beth-shemesh being absent. Beth-shemesh is not mentioned in the Bible after the days of Ahaz (2 Chr. 28:18), but according to archaeological research the city existed until the fall of the kingdom of Judah.[44] Therefore the absence of Beth-shemesh does not prevent us from dating the list of Aaronite cities to the same period as the province list. Two of the four towns of Benjamin, Geba and Gibeon, are also mentioned in the province list of Judah (Josh. 18:21-28). Anathoth is well known in the time of the Monarchy and

43. Noth, *Josua*, p. 132.

44. G.E. Wright, "Beth-shemesh", *EAEHL*, vol. 1 (Jerusalem 1975), pp. 252-253.

Alemeth is mentioned together with it in the genealogy of Benjamin (1 Chr. 7:8).[45] Also, Iron Age I-II pottery was discovered in an area survey at Khirbet 'Almit, the site identified with biblical Alemeth.[46] Hence the towns of Benjamin also present no problem in dating the list of Levitical cities. Following Alt, we date the province list of the kingdom of Judah to the time of Josiah, shortly before the destruction of the kingdom.[47] We suggest, moreover, that the list of 13

45. Z. Kallai, "Almon, Alemeth", "Anathoth", *EM,* vol. 6 (1971), pp. 233-234, 318-319 [Hebrew], with further literature. Kallai (*Tribes,* pp. 336-337) has pointed out that several Benjaminite towns situated in the hill country east of the watershed are missing from the town list of Benjamin in Josh. 18:21-28 (e.g., Anathoth, Alemeth, Michmash, Nob and perhaps Gibeah of Benjamin). He thinks that an entire district was mistakenly omitted in the transmission of the text. However, the area is too small for a district and the missing towns were probably originally part of the southern Benjaminite district (Josh. 18:25-28), which would thus have been roughly the same size as its southern neighbour, the district of Bethlehem. Might one suggest that in 18:25-28 due to homoioteleuton, the names between Gibeah (of Benjamin) and Gibeah (of Kiriath-jearim) were omitted?

46. Kallai, in: Kochavi, *Judaea,* p. 187 no. 152.

47. Alt, "Judas Gaue", pp. 100-111 [=*KS,* vol. 2, pp. 276-284]. Alt's dating is supported by the names in the Benjaminite town list (Josh. 18:23-24). The naming of places according to the ethnic group or origin of the inhabitants is a well-known phenomenon in the ancient Near East (e.g., Jebus for Jerusalem). See also: I. Eph'al, "The Western Minorities in Babylonia in the 6th-5th

Aaronite cities should also be dated to the time of Josiah, and that the complete system of Levitical cities was likewise composed at the same time.

The question of Levitical cities inhabited by Aaronites, as well as the appearance of the term 'Levitical city' (or, for that matter 'cities of priests') should be discussed briefly. The presence of Levite families in the tribe of Judah and the other south Judaean tribes is known from the early days of the history of the people of Israel.[48] The appearance of Libnah

Centuries B.C.: Maintenance and Cohesion", *Orientalia,* vol. 47 (1978), pp. 76-87; R. Zadok, "Phoenicians, Philistines and Moabites in Mesopotamia", *BASOR,* no. 230 (1978), pp. 57-62). The Avvim (Josh. 18:23) is a place-name, called after a group of exiles brought by Sargon II from Avva, east of the Tigris, and settled in the province of Samaria (2 Kings 17:24, 31; 18:34; 19:13), probably near Bethel (cf. 2 Kings 17:28); *kpr h'mny* (Josh. 18:24) was probably called after the exiles brought to the vicinity of Bethel from the kingdom of Ammon. These settlements of exiles cannot antedate Sargon II. To be more specific, they must have occurred after his annexation of the province of Samaria to Assyria (720 B.C.) and his deportation of people from the area east of the Tigris, following his campaigns against Babylon (710/709 B.C.).

48. K. Moehlenbrink, "Die levitischen Ueberlieferungen des Alten Testaments", *ZAW,* vol. 52 (1934), pp. 191-197; J. Liver, "Korah, Dathan and Abiram", *Scripta Hierosolymitana,* vol. 8 (1961), pp. 208-214; A. Cody, *A History of Old Testament Priesthood,* Analecta Biblica, vol. 35 (Rome 1969), pp. 158-161; J.M. Miller, "The Korahites of Southern Judah", *CBQ,* vol. 32 (1970), pp.

and Hebron as the names of Levite families in Num. 26:58, indicating the concentration of Levite families in these two cities, is noteworthy. It is also significant that Zadok, who held the office of high priest in Jerusalem in the days of David and Solomon, was of Judaean origin, probably from Hebron.[49] It is likely that Zadok's ancestors served as priests in Hebron during the premonarchial period, and that David selected a member of the priestly dynasty serving in his first capital for promotion to the high priesthood in his new capital, Jerusalem.

The early presence of Levites in Beth-shemesh cannot be inferred from 1 Sam. 6:15, since this is undoubtedly a late interpolation.[50] The city of Nob, situated in the southern territory of Benjamin, is called "the city of the priests" (1 Sam. 22:19), being inhabited in the days of Saul by priests descended from the Shiloh priesthood (1 Sam. 21:1-10; 22:9-23). After the destruction of Shiloh, other descendandts

58-68; de Vaux, *Early History*, pp. 529-534; id., *Ancient Israel*, pp. 361-371; Haran, *Temples*, pp. 71-92.

49. F.M. Cross, *Canaanite Myth and Hebrew Epic: Essays in the History of the Religion of Israel* (Cambridge Mass. 1973), pp. 207-215; Haran, *Temples*, pp. 77-78, 88.

50. See, inter alii, J. Wellhausen, *Der Text der Buecher Samuelis* (Goettingen 1871), p. 65; P. Dhorme, *Les Livre de Samuel*, Etudes Bibliques (Paris 1910), p. 61; and more recently P.K. McCarter, *I Samuel, The Anchor Bible*, vol. 8 (New York 1980), p. 136.

of Eli's family setlled in Anathoth, where Abiathar had an estate (1 Kings 2:26). The House of Eli may have affiliated itself with Aaron, though this is by no means certain.[51]

All this may indicate the early existence of cities inhabited by Levites in the neighbourhood of Hebron, as well as in the Shephelah (Libnah) and in the territory of Benjamin. Unfortunately, the pattern of settlement of the Levites in this early period, the time of the United Monarchy, remains unknown.

The 'cities of the priests' of the Judaean kingdom in the days of Hezekiah, recorded in 2 Chr. 31:14-19, are also of interest. The concept of cities of the priests and the Levites is typical of the Chronicler, appearing several times in his book (1 Chr. 6:54-81 [= MT 6:39-66] ; 13:2; 2 Chr. 11:13-16). According to him they were settlements in which the families of the priests and Levites lived, which was certainly the situation prevailing in his own time, i.e., the Persian period (cf. Neh. 11:20; 12:28-29). It is unlikely that the families of priests and Levites, returning from Babylon to Judah, would have received estates and pasture lands if they did not have hereditary titles. The description of Hezekiah's arrangements was thus apparently based on the reality of the time of the

51. Haran, *Temples,* pp. 87, 99; J. Liver, "Eli, the Sons of Eli", *EM,* vol. 6 (1971), pp. 231-233 [Hebrew]. For a different opinion, see Cross, op.cit. [note 49 above], pp. 195-206; Halpern, op.cit. [note 9 above], pp. 31-42.

Monarchy, although the text bears the stamp of the Chronicler. These arrangements probably remained untouched by the reform of Josiah. Josiah's action recorded in 2 Kings 23:8 ("And he brought all the priests out of the cities of Judah...") marked the end of the priesthood of Levites in the cities of Judah, and the centralization of the cult in Jerusalem, but not the concentration of all priests and their families in the capital.

One may conclude that the picture of scattered towns inhabited by the Levites reflects the reality of the Judaean kingdom in the time of the Monarchy. Several of these towns had already contained groups of Levites in the time of the United Monarchy (Hebron, Libnah, Anathoth and perhaps others). The 13 towns inhabited by the Aaronites, however, probably represent the reality of the 7th century B.C. This picture seems to have influenced decisively what happened in Judah following the Babylonian captivity.

It is now possible to propose a hypothesis for the motivation of the author of the system of Levitical cities, and for the way in which he formulated his composition. The extension of Judaean rule under Josiah to regions once belonging to the kingdom of Israel and the extensive reform – which led to Jerusalem's becoming the exclusive cultic centre of Judah – brought with it a widespread consciousness of the inauguration of a new era, and a feeling of restoration of former glory. This period, at the end of the 7th century B.C., was thus a suitable time for the composition of a system in which all twelve Israelite tribes would be represented, extending to their maximum boundaries of the days of David and Solomon.

The concept of Levitical cities was based on the reality of the Aaronite cities in the kingdom of Judah in the author's time. These 13 cities lay in the territory of three tribes – Judah, Simeon and Benjamin. It was this situation that suggested to the author the scheme of four cities per tribe and three tribes per clan of Levites. Around the Aaronite nucleus the writer wove a framework of cities associating the dwelling places of the priests and Levites with arrangements ostensibly made immediately after the Israelite occupation of the land. This he presented as a system embracing the twelve tribes of Israel.

The historical reality of the geographical division of the Levitical cities among the three families of the Kohathites, Gershonites and Merarites is not easy to determine. Why did the author connect a family of Levites with a particular region? Here we must state an important methodological principle: even if someone is writing a hypothetical composition, he finds it easier to base himself on genuine foundations. However, our knowledge of the seats of Levite families on both sides of the Jordan is scanty and we can only make a few suggestions.

According to Judg. 18:30, the sons of Gershom, son of Moses, were priests in the temple of Dan "until the day of the captivity of the land". Let us assume that the author of the system identified Gershom son of Moses with Gershon son of Levi. It may then be suggested that since the Gershonite families were scattered in various Galilean localities, the author decided to connect most of the cities of the Gershonites with this region.[52] We also know that Levite families, descended according to tradition from Aaron, served at Shiloh and Bethel in the time of the Judges. Shiloh and Bethel being in the inheritance of Ephraim are both part of the House of Joseph. Since Aaron and Moses were regarded in the late tradition as grandsons of Kohath, the author may have connected the Levitical cities located in the territory of the House of Joseph with the rest of the sons of Kohath. On the other hand, there is a clear contradiction between the tradition that the Kohathite family of Hebron was transferred to the area of Gad and Reuben, including the city of Jaazer (1 Chr. 26:30-32), and the system of Levitical cities, where it is the sons of Merari who appear in that area.[53]

52. Noth, *Josua,* p. 132. On the confusion between the families of Gershom son of Moses and Gershon son of Levi, see also S.E. Loewenstamm, "The Sons of Gershom, the Sons of Gershon", *EM,* vol. 2 (1954), p. 567 [Hebrew].

53. The verses relating to the service of the Kohathite family of Hebron in Transjordan (1 Chr. 26:30-32) were regarded by Mazar ("Levites", pp. 197-199) as the key to the correct interpretation of the system of Levitical cities. Curiously enough, he did not notice the obvious contradiction between these verses and the system itself.

The conclusions reached in this chapter have far-reaching consequences for the history of the priests and Levites in the time of the Monarchy and for the evaluation of the Priestly Code as an historical source. The interpretation of the system of Levitical cities as an authentic historical document was taken as proof that one of the schematic and symmetrical descriptions so common in the Priestly Code is authentic and concrete, thus giving encouragement to those scholars who were trying to claim the authenticity of other schematic descriptions. Our presentation of the system of Levitical cities as an artificial 'literary' composition, lacking any historical significance, changes the balance of the evidence and obliges us to investigate these problems anew.

Should our conclusions – that the list of Levitical cities is to be dated to the end of the 7th century B.C., and that its historical kernel included only 13 Judaean cities – be correct, the cornerstone of many studies of the history of the Levites in the time of the Monarchy has been removed. The entire picture will have to be modified.

CHAPTER SEVEN

THE PLACE OF THE SINAI PENINSULA IN EGYPTIAN AND BIBLICAL BORDER CONCEPTS

1) Introduction

The modern concept of international borders is a clear-cut line separating neighbouring countries and passing through different types of terrain, which may include deserts and mountains, rivers and lakes. In ancient times, the same kind of demarcation was used to delineate densely-populated areas, because villages, fields and sources of water needed to be accurately marked in order to establish ownership. There were, however, other areas where exact demarcation of the border had no practical significance. This was the case in unoccupied and uncultivated territory such as waterless deserts, steep mountains and forests. How was such territory regarded by two rulers between whose kingdoms it lay?

The Sinai Peninsula is an excellent example.[1] On its western side was the delta of the Nile, and on its northern side the Land of Canaan. Egypt and Canaan were two totally different civilizations, each with its own history, culture and political organization. Even during the 400 years when Canaan was under Egypt's rule it was not incorporated by the Pharaohs, who made no attempt to impose an overall Egyptian system of administration.[2] The permanent occupation of Canaan gave the Pharaohs certain political, strategic and economic advantages, but Egypt and Canaan remained separate entities, largely because of the wide uninhabited expanse lying between their settled areas. Sinai was a buffer zone between two countries and

1. This chapter is partly based on two articles published by the present writer: "Brook" and "Shihor", and the reader is referred to the extensive bibliography cited at the end of each. See also: A. Sneh, T. Weissbrod and I. Perath, "Evidence for an Ancient Egyptian Frontier Canal", *American Scientist,* vol. 63 (1975), pp. 542-548; W.H. Shea, "A Date for the Recently Discovered Eastern Canal of Egypt", *BASOR,* no. 226 (1977), pp. 31-38.

2. The intensification of the Egyptian occupation of Canaan and the annexation of considerable territory in southern Canaan during the time of the 19th-20th Dynasties may well have caused changes in this picture. See A. Alt, "Aegyptische Tempel in Palaestina und die Landnahme der Philister", *ZDPV,* vol. 67 (1944), pp. 1-20 [= *KS,* vol. 1, pp. 216-230]; J.M. Weinstein, "The Egyptian Empire in Palestine: A Reassessment", *BASOR,* no. 241 (1981), pp. 17-23.

two civilizations, and the definition of a border posed a special problem for scribes on both sides.

We shall first review the Egyptian attitude to the Sinai Peninsula as reflected in sources dated to the second millennium B.C., and then the biblical concept of it.

2) The Egyptian View of the Eastern Border

The eastern border of Egypt was marked by the Eastern Canal of the delta throughout the second millennium B.C. In the time of the Middle Kingdom (1991-1786 B.C.), fortresses were built along this line to defend Egypt against desert nomads. The line was called The Wall of the Ruler, both in the story of Sinuhe and in the Prophecy of Neferti.[3]

When Sinuhe returned to Egypt from Asia, he was escorted by Asiatics to The Ways of Horus.[4] In the documents of the New Kingdom, this was a name for Sile, possibly located in the vicinity of Tell Abu Seifeh, east of Qantarah.[5] "The

3. J. A. Wilson, in: *ANET*, pp. 19a and 446a.

4. Wilson, ibid., p. 21b.

5. For the identification of Sile with Tell Abu Seifeh, see Gardiner, "Road", pp. 104-106, 115; id., *Ancient Egyptian Onomastica*, vol. 1 (Oxford 1947), p. 181*; vol. 2, pp. 202*-203*. However, the recent archaeological survey conducted in that area has demonstrated that Tell Abu Seifeh was not built before the Persian period. Sile should probably be located in one of the New

fortress of The Ways of Horus" appears as the first station on the way to Gaza in a papyrus of the 19th Dynasty.[6] Sile was the first station on the way to Gaza both in the annals of Thutmes III and in the legend accompanying the Seti I reliefs depicting the stations on the road from Egypt to Canaan.[7] "The fortress of Ramesses which is in Sile" is mentioned as a point of departure to Canaan in a 'model letter' from the time of Ramesses II.[8] The city of Pi-Ramesse, the Delta capital of the Ramessides, was described as "the forefront of every foreign land and the end of Egypt".[9]

Kingdom settlements discovered in this region. See. E.D. Oren, "North Sinai Survey 1972-1978", in: *Sinai in Antiquity: Researches in the History and Archaeology of the Peninsula,* eds. Z. Meshel and I. Finkelstein (Tel Aviv 1980), pp. 124, 157 n. 70 [Hebrew].

6. Gardiner, "Road", pp. 103-106, 115-116; Helck, *Beziehungen,* pp. 310-311.

7. Wilson, op. cit. [note 3 above], p. 235a; Gardiner, "Road", pp. 99-101; Helck, *Beziehungen,* pp. 311-313.

8. Gardiner, "Road", pp. 106-107.

9. A.H. Gardiner, *Late-Egyptian Miscellanies,* Bibliotheca Aegyptiaca, vol. 7 (Bruxelles 1937), p. 28 lines 11-12; R.A. Caminos, *Late-Egyptian Miscellanies* (London 1954), p. 101 (=Papyrus Anastasi III, 7,4).

It seems a justifiable conclusion that the Eastern Canal, with the frontier fortress at Sile, demarcated the eastern boundary of Egypt, while the Sinai Peninsula was considered part of Asia. That is why the desert of Sinai was sometimes regarded as an integral part of Canaan. Thus, the route from Sile to Gaza was designated "the [foreign countries] of the end of the land of the Canaan".[10] And a scribe of the 19th Dynasty bore the title "envoy of the king to all the rulers of the foreign lands of Huru from Sile to Upi".[11]

Other Egyptian sources regarded Gaza and wadi Besor as the southern limit of Canaan. Gaza is mentioned in the annals of Thutmes III as the first place in Canaan after leaving Sile. Wishing to emphasize the extent of the rebellion confronting him, he used the phrase "from Yurza to the ends of the land". Yurza was the southernmost city of Canaan, and was situated on wadi Besor.[12]

Gaza also appears as the southern coastal city of Canaan in the sources of the 19th Dynasty describing the road from Egypt to Asia. According to Papyrus Anastasi I, this route began at Sile and ended at Gaza, with Raphia as the penultimate

10. Wilson, op. cit. [note 3 above] p. 478b.

11. Gardiner, op. cit. [note 9 above], p. 21 lines 6-7; Caminos, op. cit. [note 9 above], p. 69 (=Papyrus Anastasi III, 1, 9-10).

12. Na'aman, "Brook", pp. 74-75.

station. The same road is depicted on the reliefs of Seti I as starting at Sile and terminating at Raphia. The accompanying inscription states that in his first year, Seti smote the Shosu from the fortress of Sile to *p3 kn'n* (=Gaza). Next to the inscription, the city of Gaza is depicted as the first city of Canaan.[13]

The conception of Gaza and Yurza as part of the southernmost border of Canaan is also confirmed by archaeological finds. A line of fortified cities of the Middle Bronze Age IIB was found along the banks of wadi Besor, three in its western stretches (Tell el-'Ajjul, Tel Gamma and Tell el-Far'ah), and one in the Beer-sheba valley to the east (Tel Malḥata). Only the three western sites survived until the beginning of the Late Bronze Age. Tel Malḥata had been abandoned, and with the destruction of Tell el-'Ajjul (Sharuhen),[14] the city of Gaza replaced it as the most prominent city in the area.

The line of three southern cities (Gaza, Tel Gamma and Tell el-Far'ah) endured throughout the Late Bronze Age, and it is important to note that there was no Canaanite city south of

13. Gardiner, "Road", pp. 99-101; Wilson, op.cit. [note 3 above], p. 254b.

14. For the transcription of the name of the Hyksos city as Shir/lhon and its distinction from the biblical city of Sharuhen/Shilhim, see Na'aman, "Simeon", pp. 147-148.

this line. Several important sites have been discovered south of wadi Besor, from Deir el-Balaḥ to Sheikh ez-Zuweid (Tell er-Ridan, Raphia and Tell Abu Seleimeh). The material culture of these sites, however, was of mixed Egyptian-Canaanite character, and according to the sources cited above they were regarded not as Canaanite, but as belonging to the settlements of northern Sinai.[15] The pattern of settlement created in the Middle Bronze Age IIB, when wadi Besor was the southern limit of urban culture in Canaan, existed until the end of the second millennium B.C. The annals of Thutmes III recording rebellion "from Yurza to the end of the land" are referring to this array of urban settlements.

There is no real contradiction between the two Egyptian views. The Sinai Peninsula was consistently regarded as part of Asia and was never included within the boundaries of the land of Egypt. As contacts between Egypt and Canaan increased and the Egyptians became more familiar with conditions to the

15. For the sites discovered in the survey recently conducted in northern Sinai, see Oren, op. cit. [note 5 above], pp. 109-114; id., "An Egyptian Fort on the Military Route to Canaan", *Qadmoniot*, vol. 6 (1973), pp. 101-103 [Hebrew]; id., "Egyptian New Kingdom Sites in North-Eastern Sinai", *Qadmoniot*, vol. 13 (1980), pp. 26-33 [Hebrew]; Trude Dothan, *Excavations at the Cemetery of Deir el-Balaḥ*, Qedem, vol. 10 (1979); id., "Deir el-Balaḥ 1979-1980", *IEJ*, vol. 31 (1981), pp. 126-131; A. Biran, "Tell er-Ridan", *IEJ*, vol. 24 (1974), p. 142; cf. W.M.F. Petrie and J.C. Ellis, *Anthedon, Sinai* (London 1937), p. 8.

north-east, they also became aware that the Sinai Peninsula was not part of Canaan. Thus, when their scribes were dealing exclusively with Canaan, they took its border to be the southernmost limit of the array of city-states in the region, with Sinai a no-man's-land between Egypt and the inhabited areas of Canaan.

3) The Biblical Concept of the Southern Border

In the Bible, two basic concepts of the border are described in great detail:[16]

(a) The Land of Canaan (Num. 34; Ezek. 47). This reflects the political situation and pattern of settlement of the second millennium B.C. This long-established concept of the land, including its southern border, was adopted by the Israelites from the local Canaanite population.

(b) The tribal inheritances (Josh. 13-19). These reflect the confines of the United Monarchy at its peak. The boundary system applied only to Israelite territory; the areas of the neighbouring vassal states (Philistia, Tyre, Sidon, Aram, Ammon, Moab, Edom) remained outside it [see chapter 1 pp. 60-63, 72].

In addition to these two detailed descriptions, there is a third and broader notion: the 'Patriarchs' borders' (Gen.

16. Na'aman, "Shihor", pp. 96-98, with further literature.

15:18, extending "from the river of Egypt to the great river, the river Euphrates". These borders do not belong to the same category as the other two, for they are defined only by the 'from... to...' formula. Furthermore, it is my opinion that this idea could not possibly have developed before the whole area had come to be regarded as a single unit. This happened at the beginning of the 7th century B.C., with the unification of all the territory from the Euphrates to Egypt under the hegemony of Assyria, and the resulting administrative term *eber nari* (Beyond the River). The 'Patriarchs' borders' embodies the promise that the territory of the Israelite nation will one day extend over the whole of *eber nari,* from the Euphrates to the Nile. This biblical notion was a foreign one, and has no basis in the actual history of the country. It is therefore irrelevant to the present discussion.

As there were two basic biblical concepts of the southern border, so there were two different demarcations of it [see chapter 1 pp. 62-66]. The first, crossing from the Dead Sea to Wadi Besor, is the southern boundary of the historical Land of Canaan, corresponding to the southernmost limits of urban settlement in the second millennium B.C. (e.g., Gen 10:19; Num. 21:1; 33:40; 1 Kings 4:24 [= MT 5:4]). The second border, that of the tribal allotments, reached the Negeb highlands and Kadesh-barnea, the southernmost settlement in the time of the United Monarchy. These two border lines reflect completely different political situations and patterns of settlement. In neither case was the Sinai Peninsula regarded as part of the inhabited country to the north of it.

We may therefore regard the biblical concepts as the 'northern' point of view, reflecting both the Canaanite and the Israelite ideas of the border. For these peoples, the southernmost line of urban settlement marked their border and they – unlike the Egyptians – regarded Sinai as part of the land of Egypt.

This requires some explanation. Generally, when borders are demarcated in the Bible, no territorial gaps are left between countries. Neighbouring kingdoms were considered to extend right to the boundaries of the Israelite kingdom; the allotment of the land among the twelve tribes covered the entire country, and even non-settled areas or Canaanite enclaves were included. In the same way, the whole Israelite kingdom was divided among the twelve Solomonic districts (1 Kings 4:7-19). That is why the biblical authors regarded the area south of the country as part of Egypt, just as the Egyptians looked upon the area east of their country as part of Asia. This, in my opinion, is the origin of the name Brook of Egypt: it was the river demarcating the border with Egypt from the point of view of the people living north-east of it.

The Brook of Egypt is mentioned six times in the Bible, always with reference to the southern border of the country. Some years ago, I suggested that the Brook of Egypt was wadi Besor. Only after the destruction and abandonment of the land following the fall of Jerusalem, and the ensuing change in the pattern of settlement in northern Sinai during the Persian period, was the old tradition forgotten and the Brook of Egypt considered to be Wadi el-'Arish.[17] This theory is supported by the fact that the component 'Egypt' was used in the name designating the southern border of the land. And when one compares 1 Kings 4:21 [= MT 5:1], "Solomon ruled over all the kingdoms from the Euphrates... to the border of Egypt" with 1 Kings 8:65, "So Solomon held the feast at that time, and all Israel with him... from the entrance of Hamath to the Brook of Egypt...", it is obvious that the Brook of Egypt corresponded with the border of Egypt.

Two biblical toponyms, Shihor and Shur, are said to be *'l pny mṣrym* (opposite Egypt). This phrase conveys the same idea as the Brook of Egypt. All three names refer to the boundary between the Israelite kingdom and Egypt. It seems to me that the passages in Josh. 13:3 and 1 Chr. 13:5, mentioning Shihor in border descriptions refer to the Brook of Egypt and not to a branch of the Nile.[18] It is also my opinion that Shur was the name of an important site on the main route leading north from Kadesh-barnea, probably to be identified with Tell el-Far'ah, situated by wadi Besor.[19]

17. For a discussion of the location of the Brook of Egypt, see Na'aman, "Brook", criticised by A.F. Rainey, "Toponymic Problems (cont.): The Brook of Egypt", *Tel Aviv*, vol. 9 (1982), pp. 131-132.

18. For a comprehensive discussion of the location of Shihor, see Na'aman, "Shihor", pp. 96-100, with further literature.

19. Na'aman, "Shihor", pp. 100-105, with further literature.

The Brook of Egypt is also mentioned in the Assyrian royal inscriptions from the time of Tiglath-pileser III, Sargon II and Esarhaddon, always signifying the southern limit of Assyrian power on the Egyptian front.[20] The inscriptions obviously reflect the same 'northern' point of view as we have seen in the Bible.

Siruati the Me'unite was situated, according to a 'summary inscription' of Tiglath-pileser III, "below (i.e., at the foot of) Egypt".[21] The Me'unites lived in the territory adjacent to wadi Besor (cf. 1 Chr. 4:39-41), and this area was regarded by the Assyrian scribe as being 'at the foot of Egypt'. According to another 'summary inscription', Tiglath-pileser III entrusted the Arab tribe Idibi'ilu with the task of 'gatekeeping over Egypt' following the conquest of Ashkelon.[22] It is obvious that the Assyrian scribes regarded the area south of the coast of Philistia as the gate of Egypt.

Finally, we may note the new suggestion that the 'sealed harbour of Egypt' mentioned by Sargon II should be located at Tell Abu Seleimeh, near Sheikh ez-Zuweid.[23] If this is

20. Na'aman, "Brook", pp. 68-74; id., "Shihor", p. 105.

21. Na'aman, "Brook", p. 69, with further literature.

22. Na'aman, "Brook", pp. 69-70, with further literature.

23. R. Reich, "The identification of the 'Sealed *karu* of Egypt'", *IEJ*, vol. 34 (1984), pp. 32-38.

acceptable, it adds further evidence that the area south of wadi Besor was regarded by the Assyrians as part of Egypt.[24]

We have shown that the concepts of the southern border of the land in the Bible and in the Assyrian royal inscriptions are all remarkably consistent. The Brook of Egypt, Shihor [25] and Shur are all placed at the southern limit of the country, and beyond this, without any gap, the territory of Egypt begins.

It is perhaps of interest that in the description of the Exodus, the perspective and the terms used are those of people coming out of Egypt, towards the Land of Canaan.

Calling the Sile - Gaza road the "...way of the land of the Philistines..." (Ex. 13:17) is looking at it from Egypt. Also Migdol (Ex. 14:2; Num. 33:7), which is mentioned in the tradition of the Exodus, seems to be identical with the 'Migdol

24. The identification of the 'sealed harbour of Egypt' at Tell Abu Seleimeh may corroborate our identification of the Brook of Egypt with wadi Besor. Though Tell Abu Seleimeh is located north of Wadi el-'Arish, it was regarded by the Assyrians as part of Egypt. This would mean that the northern border of Egypt was located north of it, i.e., at wadi Besor. This holds even if we identify the 'sealed harbour' with Tell er-Ruqeish, situated south of wadi Besor. There, a large harbour has been uncovered, dated to the 7th century B.C., and probably established by the Assyrians.

25. This holds for Josh. 13:3 and 1 Chr. 13:5; on the other hand, in Isa. 23:3 and Jer. 2:18, Shihor is another name for the Nile.

of Menma're' mentioned in the series of reliefs of Pharaoh Seti I.[26] Although the location of other toponyms recalled in the traditions of the Exodus is disputed, it seems clear that the boundary of Egypt reflected in those descriptions is identical to the borderline as conceived by the Egyptians themselves.

In the biblical tradition, the sojourn of the Israelites in the Sinai desert was regarded as an interlude outside the border of Canaan. Even their stay at Kadesh-barnea, which according to some traditions marked the southernmost border of both Canaan and the tribe of Judah (Num. 34:4; Josh. 15:3; Ezek. 47:19), was regarded as a sojourn outside the borders of Canaan (cf. Ex. 16:35; Josh. 5:12). It was from Kadesh-barnea that the spies were sent to scout out the land and the unsuccessful attempt to enter Canaan from the south began (Num. 13-14). In this tradition, the biblical Negeb (i.e., the Beer-sheba valley) was regarded as the most southerly region of Canaan (Gen. 10:19; 13:1; Num. 13:17, 22, 29; 21:1; Judg. 1:9), whereas the oasis of Kadesh-barnea was considered part of the desert beyond it (Gen. 16:7; 21:14; Num. 13:26; 1 Kings 19:3-4). This accords wel with the fact that the limits of the urban settlements marked the boundary of the Land of Canaan. In the traditions of the Exodus and the desert wanderings,

26. Gardiner, "Road", pp. 107-108; Helck, *Beziehungen,* p. 311. For the site of the city of Migdol, mentioned by Jeremiah (44:1; 46:14) and Ezekiel (29:10; 30:6), see E.D. Oren, "'Migdol' Fortress in North Western Sinai", *Qadmoniot,* vol. 10 (1977), pp. 71-76 [Hebrew].

the Sinai Peninsula was not envisaged as part either of Egypt or of Canaan.

To sum up: the Egyptians and the biblical writers treat the Sinai Peninsula in exactly the same manner. When they describe their own boundaries, they both regard the Sinai desert as being outside their territory and belonging to the other country. However, when they are talking about the Sinai per se, and not in connection with their own borders, they regard it as no-man's-land.

It seems justifiable to assume that this attitude to uninhabited desert areas is a general one, common to all cultivated and populated lands in the ancient Near East.

INDEX OF BIBLICAL PASSAGES

INDEX OF AUTHORS

INDEX OF GEOGRAPHICAL NAMES

תוכן עניינים

ספרים קודמים בסדרת עיונים במקרא ובתקופתו:

א: א. רופא, ספר בלעם.

ב: טליה רודין־אוברסקי, מאלוני ממרא עד סדום.

ג: ע. טוב, תרגום השבעים ככלי עזר במחקר המקרא. [אנגלית]

נדפס בדפוס יובל, ירושלים

עיונים במקרא ובתקופתו

ד

גבולות ונחלות בהיסטוריוגרפיה המקראית
הרשימות הגיאוגרפיות במקרא
שבעה מחקרים

מאת

נדב נאמן

הוצאת סימור בע"מ
ירושלים תשמ"ו

עיונים במקרא ובתקופתו

בעריכת

אורה ליפשיץ ואלכסנדר רופא

סדרת "עיונים במקרא ובתקופתו" נועדה להגיש לציבור הלומדים מחקרים בשאלות ספרות המקרא והתהוותה, אמונת ישראל ותולדות ימי קדם.

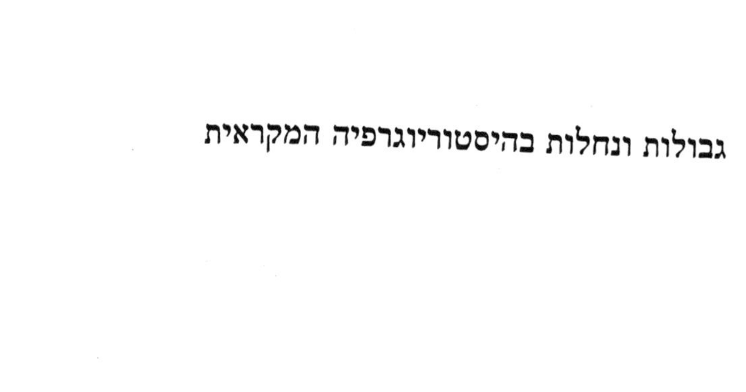

גבולות ונחלות בהיסטוריוגרפיה המקראית